Managing Successful Requirements Projects:

The Analyst's Playbook

Trond Frantzen

Cataloguing-in-Publication Data

Copyright © 2024 **Trond Frantzen**.

Managing Successful Requirements Projects: The Analyst's Playbook

1. Project management
2. Requirements elicitation
3. Business analysis
4. System analysis
5. Agile
6. Structured
7. Systems
8. IT projects
9. Process modeling

Cover Design: Owais Ashraf

All rights reserved. The material contained in this publication is protected under the copyright laws of the United States, Canada and Internationally. This material cannot be reproduced in any form or by any means without written permission from the author. Any infringement of these copyrights or trademarks can be prosecuted to the full extent of the law.

You can reach Trond Frantzen at the address below:

Trond.PowerstartGroup@gmail.com

trondfrantzen.com

Managing Successful Requirements Projects:

The Analyst's Playbook

Trond Frantzen

Table of Contents

About the Author	10
Introduction ...	12
Preface	16
Book I: What is Business System Analysis?	19
System Development Methodologies	22
The Pitfalls of Conventional Analysis Methods and Management	50
The Professional's Project Success Code	53
Book II: The 5-Point Project Plan	57
1. Initiate & Plan (Intro)	58
2. Conduct Project Scope Blitz (Intro)	59
3. Plan Detailed Discovery Sessions (Intro)	60
4. Conduct Detailed Discovery Sessions (Intro)	60
5. Coordinate Business Analysis Completion (Intro)	61
1. Initiate & Plan	62
Identifying Key Roles	62
Defining Assignment	63
Setting Metrics for Success	65
Listing Deliverables and Artifacts	67
Outcome: **Business Analysis Plan**	69
2. Conduct Project Scope Blitz	71
Organizing the Scope Blitz	72
Engaging Stakeholders and SMEs	72
Creating the Project Business Event List	73
Setting the Tone for the Project	73
Outcome: **Project Business Event List**	74

	Guiding Subsequent Activities	74
	Supporting Decision-Making	75
	Facilitating Communication and Collaboration	75
3.	Plan Detailed Discovery Sessions	76
	Establishing a Structured Approach	77
	Creating the Schedule	77
	Aligning with Project Objectives	77
	Leveraging Standard Metrics	78
	Managing Flexibility and Adaptability	78
	Allocating Time and Resources	78
	Engaging SMEs and Stakeholders	79
	Facilitating Collaboration and Communication	79
	Outcome: **Project Discovery Schedule**	80
	Dynamic and Iterative Planning	80
	Ensuring Comprehensive Coverage	80
	Facilitating Stakeholder Engagement	80
4.	Conduct Detailed Discovery Sessions	81
	Inviting SMEs	82
	Conducting the Sessions	82
	Completing Documentation	83
	Outcome: **Project Business Requirements**	83
	Cultivating a Culture of Continuous Improvement	84
5.	Coordinate Business Analysis Completion	84
	Managing the Project Phases	85
	Coordinating with the Technology Team	85
	Documenting Lessons Learned	85
	Outcome: **Business Analysis Project Review**	86

Leveraging Agile Methodologies	86
Cultivating Cross-Functional Collaboration	87
Prioritizing Stakeholder Engagement	87

The 5-Point Project Plan – Conclusion	88
Review – The 5-Point Project Plan	89

Book III: How to Run Awesome Business Discovery Sessions — 93

What's this all about?	95
What is a business discovery session?	96
What's a business discovery session good for?	96
The risks and rewards of business discovery sessions	98
The benefits of business discovery sessions	98
What is … the projects cope blitz?	100
And … what is a business discovery session?	101
How long does a discovery session take?	102
The project scope blitz	102
The business discovery session	106
How much time is needed for a project's business requirements?	109
What kind of facility is required?	110
Who should participate?	111
Who should participate? – the Pilot	112
Who should participate? – the Co-Pilot	114
Who should participate – the Coach	115
Who should participate? – Executive Sponsors and Project Primes	115
Who should participate? – Subject-Matter Experts and other Business Partners	116
Why do we need to do this?	116
What do business discovery sessions accomplish?	117
So, what is a business event?	119
The four types of business events	120
The symbiotic relationship between objects and processes	122
And then we're done …	126

Three important things: First …	127
Three important things: Second …	128
Three important things: Third …	128
What tools can you use for documentation?	129
Key success factors	131
Business discovery session tips and techniques	136
On the Co-Pilot	139
After the Discovery Sessions	142
Other thoughts on business discovery sessions	143
More tips and techniques	144
The Agile environment	148
The Professional's Success Code (Revisited)	151

Conclusion   152

About the Author

Trond Frantzen is a business development strategist, an analyst, and a business executive. He is the Managing Partner of the PowerStart Group, a boutique consulting firm that focuses on business growth, sustainability consulting, and development solutions for emerging businesses.

Trond has delivered strategic consulting services to scores of clients in the United States, Canada, the U.K., and Europe. He has led interactive business system development sessions with over 35,000 client staff. He is the author of several business analysis books, along with his environmental sustainability books.

Trond was born in Norway, raised in Toronto's west end, graduated from Concordia University where he studied Computer Science and Environmental Science, lives in Calgary (Canada), and is connected to a large social network of friends and acquaintances.

Trond has been recognized as a finalist in the Oakville (Ontario) *Entrepreneur of the Year* Awards for Business Excellence, in addition to being recognized by many professional associations.

You can connect with Trond on LinkedIn at http://www.linkedin.com/in/trondfrantzen or you can email him at trond.powerstartgroup@gmail.com

You can find some of his other books at: **trondfrantzen.com**

Books by Trond Frantzen

Business System Analysis

- Managing Successful Requirements Projects: The Analyst's Playbook
- Agile Business Requirements Analysis
- How to Run Awesome Business Discovery Sessions
- Business Requirements Analysis Made Easy
- Mastering Business Requirements Analysis
- Process Modeling for Business Analysts Made Easy
- Requirements Analysis for Non-Technical Business Analysts
- Business System Analysis for IT Consultants
- Rapid Business System Analysis: The Course
- Rapid, Agile Business System Analysis
- How to Run Awesome Discovery Sessions
- A Game Plan for System Development (with Ken McEvoy)

Environment, Social, and Governance

- Your Politician & The Environment: How to Build a Sustainable Future (The Fight for Our Lives #3)
- Politics vs. Planet: The Battle for a Sustainable Future (The Fight for Our Lives #2)
- Clean Energy & Technology Innovation – and the Environment: Are They Sustainable? (The Fight for Our Lives #1)
- ESG: From Acronym to Action (with Chris D. Tesarski)

Introduction ...

My longstanding passion for business system analysis began decades ago when I ran into my first problems with program specifications. Yes, back in the day, it was all about programs, not so much about "systems". And anything that wasn't a program spec was always pretty vague.

With today's approach to system building, it seems we have returned to focusing on programs (now mostly known as *apps*), and not so much on systems. But I digress.

In the early part of my career, I was a programmer, and a pretty good one too. I learned several programming languages that were popular at the time. I became fascinated by databases – a somewhat esoteric idea at the time, since most "databases" were pretty basic. Not too fancy. And pretty clunky.

I soon discovered the concept of the *relational data model*, which was ignored by most, as it was perceived to be (a) academic, and therefore of little practical value; (b) too geeky even for programmers, who were totally thought of as geeks working silently with their esoteric code; and (c) simply too difficult to wrap your head around.

So, while most of my programming peers looked elsewhere for data design ideas, I took on the challenge of understanding the relational data model in all its academic glory.

It was painful.

After much experimentation, including dead ends and unproductive forays into bright ideas that went nowhere, I finally had an epiphany and arrived at an understanding.

That understanding of the relational data model and accompanying rules of data normalization, however, led to a radical restructuring of how I thought we should approach system analysis. This eventually led to what I've come to call the **PowerStart Event-Based Approach to Business System Analysis**. No, there is no acronym. Mostly, it's known as the **PowerStart Analysis Approach**. I've written several books about this approach to business system analysis, and our company has used it with great success on over 850 projects of all sizes.

Somewhere along this road, being involved in many projects personally, I found that clients and project managers rarely (if ever) had a meaningful plan for the business analysis part of the project, although they put lots of effort into defining the path to follow for system design, programming, testing, and system release. But not so much for analysis.

There was also not so much of an understanding that analysis, of any kind, is highly iterative and recursive. The norm was to define front-end analysis as (a) linear, and (b) brief. This is probably because most system work of the day was also greatly serial in nature, and project work was based on a *Waterfall methodology*. However, that's not how our brains work. We jump in and out of *states*, rather than progressing serially in our analysis, and we build our understanding through recursion.

All of this, on project after project, suggested to me that a more robust front-end project plan was needed, specific to business system analysis. Also, the nature of the PowerStart Approach to business system analysis was to focus on "**what**" (the essential requirements), and not the "**how**" (which is the technology architecture, the solution design, and the details of implementation). The "what" was a fairly stable view of business requirements, while the "how" went to the often-volatile technology of the day. This approach is meant to clearly separate *how we do it* from *what data we need* to meet the business requirements. And we need a project plan for the front-end analysis.

This has led to this book on project planning and management for successful business system analysis.

But, first, a few words about this book.

A book – like all books – captures a moment in time, subject to change and evolution. I refrained from embedding reference links throughout the text for two reasons. First, Internet resources and knowledge evolve rapidly, rendering specific links obsolete. Second, I encourage you to conduct your own current research based on the foundational information provided, reinforcing your personal understanding.

As someone once said, *"Without a plan, you might end up somewhere else."* True. And, sadly, this means you'll fail in your objective. Failing, in the world of business system analysis, doesn't usually mean a crash-and-burn. It means missing some of the requirements, which often leads to high system maintenance costs and unhappy clients. It brings on a lot of *"You didn't tell me,"* from the software engineering team, and responses like, *"And you didn't ask me"* from the client.

This is not good. It's a failure of communication, and a failure to uncover and specify the full business requirements.

If you want to discuss any aspects of this book, connect with me.

Trond Frantzen
trond.powerstartgroup@gmail.com

Preface

"Data is like garbage. You'd better know what you're going to do with it before you start collecting it."

– Mark Twain –
American humorist

Since you received this book, you have probably already scanned some of the pages, and before getting into any serious reading you are wondering about its contents. I imagine that you have thought of several questions already. Let's try to anticipate some of them.

Is This Book for Me?
Maybe. If you are involved in any aspect of the process of system development, from beleaguered analyst to frustrated programmer, this book should give you strong insight into front-end project planning, and how you can make it much better. If you've never run into problems, maybe "Alice's Adventures in Wonderland" would be more appropriate.

Is This Another Book on Methodologies?
No. A Methodology (with a capital "M") is usually a pigeon-hole into which one project might fit. This book is about the cabinetry of front-end requirements analysis planning and management.

Why Should I be Interested in This Book?
With the growing complexity of systems today, we need all the help we can get. It's clear that no two projects are the same. A strategy that helps us deal with anything we might come up against is invaluable.

But Isn't This Just More Theory About Project Planning?

Yes. Until you apply it. Then it works.

But I Don't Use the "PowerStart Analysis Approach"!

Not everybody does. That doesn't change the fact that you need a strong, robust front-end plan for your project's business requirements analysis. Although I believe (would you expect anything different?) that the PowerStart Analysis Approach is a powerful tool in the system development process, this book isn't about that. It's about front-end requirements analysis planning and management – an area of work usually thought to be lacking details – and knowing where to start and what to do next.

Aren't There a Lot of Other Books Just Like This One?

Not that I'm aware of. There are books about system requirements analysis, and there are books on project planning and management. There are even books on methodologies for each of these. But not much that brings together project planning and requirements analysis. Even less than "not much". This book addresses the questions of, Where do I begin, and what do I do next? not by providing pages of checklists, or specific tools (I'm confident you know what you need), but by focusing attention on the nature of business system requirements analysis and the environment in which the requirements must be determined.

So, What Won't This Book Teach Me?

Magic and witchcraft. A cool programming language. Where to buy things cheap.

Well, What Will It Teach Me?

With luck, and some dedicated application, I hope it will show you how to think about putting together a really good, robust, actionable, and result-driven project plan for the business requirements analysis phase of your project.

Book I

What is Business System Analysis?

What is Business System Requirements Analysis?

> *"Computers are useless. They can only give you answers."*
> – Pablo Picasso –
> Spanish painter, sculptor, and theater designer

Pablo was right. Artificial Intelligence (AI) has made some progress, but a system's fundamental objective remains the same: Find an answer.

Analysts, on the other hand, are all about finding the questions. People like to give us answers – even if no question has been asked – but an analyst should always be asking, *"What is the question to which this (thing I heard) is the answer?"* Identifying and understanding the question is the key to good analysis.

Before we look at the ingredients for a robust front-end requirements analysis project plan, let's have a clear understanding of what our subject-matter is all about.

Business System Requirements Analysis (often known as *Requirements Elicitation*) is the process of researching and discovering information about what a business or organization needs from a new or enhanced system or software. It's a bit like asking for suggestions or requests from various people within the organization to figure out what functionality is necessary for a new (or enhanced) system or software. It should include business functionality outside the domain of software.

Here's how it typically works:

1. **Identify Stakeholders**: The first step is to identify all the people who will be using or affected by the new or enhanced system. This includes employees, managers, customers, and anyone else who has a stake in how the system will work. Not all aspects of a "system" is software.

2. **Request Input**: Once the stakeholders are identified, we request input from them. This is traditionally done through interviews, surveys, meetings, workshops, or other forms of communication. The goal is to understand their needs and requirements for the new or enhanced system, from a business perspective.

3. **Document Requirements**: All the input and feedback collected from stakeholders must be recorded and organized. This information forms a set of requirements that outline what the new or enhanced system should be able to do.

4. **Prioritize Requirements**: Not all requirements are equally important. Some are critical, while others are nice-to-have. It's essential to prioritize these requirements based on their importance to the business or organization.

5. **Validate**: Once the requirements are gathered and organized, they must be reviewed and validated by the stakeholders to ensure that they accurately represent their needs. This can be done in several ways.

6. **Communicate**: The requirements are communicated to the teams responsible for developing or procuring the

new or enhanced system. This ensures that the developers or vendors understand what is expected of them.

In essence, Business Requirements Analysis is the process of actively seeking input and feedback from the people who will use or be impacted by a new system. It helps ensure that the final system meets the actual needs and expectations of the organization, which is crucial for the success of any business system implementation.

On the surface this seems pretty straight-forward. Well, there's much more to be said.

System Development Methodologies

"If we teach today's students as we taught yesterday's, we rob them of tomorrow."
– John Dewey –
American philosopher and educational reformer

Yes, there are several methodologies and approaches for soliciting business system requirements. Some of them have been around since about 1975. (Yikes!) These methodologies provide structured frameworks and guidelines for gathering, documenting, and managing requirements. Many of these methodologies focus on managing requirements rather than how to actually determine the requirements. All provide a framework for project planning, although most only see front-end analysis as a brief phase before getting on with the "real work" of software development.

Some of the commonly used methodologies include:

1. **Waterfall Methodology**:
   - Using a Waterfall methodology, requirements are typically gathered upfront in a sequential manner before development begins.
   - Requirements are detailed in a Requirements Specification Document (yes, typically a conventional document!), and any changes after this stage may be costly and time-consuming.
   - Stakeholders typically make up the primary team who are involved in the initial requirement gathering phase, while only a representative cohort of subject-matter experts (SMEs) are included.

Risks of the Waterfall Methodology
The Waterfall methodology, while once widely used, has several notable risks and limitations.

1. Limited Flexibility:
Waterfall is characterized by its sequential nature, where each phase must be completed before moving on to the next. This lack of flexibility makes it difficult to accommodate changes in requirements, technology, or stakeholder priorities once the project is underway. Changes often require revisiting earlier stages, leading to potential delays and increased costs. While an iterative approach can be taken with each of the phases in a Waterfall-managed project, its nature discourages it.

2. Late Testing:

Testing typically occurs towards the end of the development cycle in Waterfall-managed projects, after the entire system has been designed and implemented. This is sometimes called "The Big Bang Approach". This can result in a situation where defects and issues related to missed requirements up-front are identified late in the process, making them very costly and time-consuming to remedy. It also increases the risk of delivering a product that does not meet client or stakeholder expectations or quality standards. There's often a lot of *"You didn't tell me,"* from the system development team, and responses like, *"And you didn't ask me"* from the client.

3. High Risk of Scope Creep:

Due to the upfront and detailed nature of requirements gathering, stakeholders may not fully understand the implications or details of their requirements until later stages. This can lead to *scope creep*, where new features or changes are requested after requirements have been finalized. Managing scope changes in Waterfall-managed projects can be challenging and often requires extensive formal change control processes. The whole issue of *scope creep* generally lacks understanding that a business unit is (and should be) dynamic and continually evolving to meet a developing business environment. Accordingly, some requirements that have been discovered after "final approval" may be quite legitimate and should be included. A Waterfall methodology does not generally support the idea that business requirements are **not** a simple snapshot in time.

4. **Customer Feedback Comes Late**:
In Waterfall-managed projects, stakeholders and end-users typically provide feedback on the product only after it has been fully developed and tested. There's usually a full-scale parallel run as the project is launched live. Waterfall-managed projects are not normally partitioned and launched in stages. This late feedback can lead to misunderstandings or mismatches between what was developed and what stakeholders actually needed or expected. Addressing feedback late in the process can be costly and may require significant rework.

5. **Long Delivery Times**:
The sequential nature of Waterfall-managed projects can result in longer delivery times compared to more iterative methodologies. Projects can experience delays if any phase takes longer than anticipated, and there is limited opportunity for early delivery of valuable functionalities to stakeholders.

6. **Less Adaptability to Change**:
In today's fast-paced and dynamic business environment, requirements and priorities can change frequently. Waterfall's rigid structure makes it less adaptable to these changes compared to agile methodologies, which emphasize iterative development and continuous feedback.

7. **Not Ideal for Complex Projects**:
Projects with high complexity may not fit well within the Waterfall framework. It can be challenging to accurately define and document all requirements upfront for such

projects – using conventional analysis tools and methods – leading to increased risk and potential project failure.

While Waterfall methodologies provides a nicely structured approach to software development (which makes us all feel better and under control), its inflexibility, late testing, risk of scope creep, and limited adaptability to change are significant downsides that can impact project success, particularly in today's dynamic and competitive business environment.

2. **Agile Methodology**:
- Agile methodologies, such as Scrum and Kanban, focus on iterative development and continuous feedback.
- Requirements are gathered in smaller increments (*epics* and *user stories*) and are refined throughout the development process.
- Stakeholder collaboration and flexibility in adapting to changing requirements are key principles of Agile.

Risks of Agile Methodologies

While Agile methodologies like Scrum and Kanban offer numerous advantages such as iterative development and flexibility, they also come with potential risks that teams need to manage effectively:

1. **Uncertainty with Scope**: The Agile approach embraces changing requirements (a good thing), which can lead to challenges in defining a clear scope from the outset (a not-so-good thing). Without a well-defined scope, teams

may struggle to manage expectations regarding what will be delivered within a given timeframe.

2. **Managing Stakeholder Expectations**: The Agile approach encourages stakeholder collaboration and continuous feedback, but this can also mean frequent changes in priorities and requirements. It may be that stakeholders are just learning about their business requirements, especially for a brand-new project or line of business, in which case this is okay. However, managing stakeholder expectations regarding what can be delivered within each iteration or *sprint* can be very challenging. Modern project management skills become very important.

3. **Resource Commitment**: Agile requires active involvement from stakeholders and the development team throughout the project. While this is a good thing, this level of commitment can be demanding and may require significant time and resources, especially in organizations new to Agile practices.

4. **Documentation Challenges**: There's no doubt that Agile projects value working software over comprehensive documentation. While this promotes efficiency and responsiveness, it can lead to gaps in documentation, which may be crucial for compliance, maintenance, or future development.

5. **Adaptation to Large Teams or Complex Projects**: Agile is highly effective for small to medium-sized teams working on projects with clear and manageable scope. However, scaling Agile practices to large teams or

complex projects requires additional coordination, communication, and possibly restructuring of workflows. This is where exceptional project management tools and techniques come into play.

6. **Dependency Management**: For Agile projects and teams, dependencies between stakeholder stories or tasks can impact the flow of work. This is especially true for projects with a great deal of cross-dependencies and recursion. Managing cross-dependencies effectively requires careful planning and coordination – exceptional project planning and execution – particularly in larger projects or those involving multiple teams.

7. **Overemphasis on Short-term Goals**: Agile projects tend to focus on delivering value in short iterations, which can sometimes lead to a myopic focus on short-term goals. This may impact long-term planning and strategic alignment, especially in projects requiring a broader vision or extensive architectural considerations. Once again, excellent project management planning and execution is required to mitigate this risk.

8. **Continuous Improvement Overload**: Agile methodologies always promote continuous improvement through extensive feedback loops. However, an out-of-balance focus on improvement can lead to constant changes in processes or tools, which may disrupt team productivity and stability. It's a risk, but a well-managed project can balance perspectives to achieve high-quality results. "High-quality results" means no business requirements missed, and successfully meeting project time and budgets.

9. **Team Member Burnout**: The iterative nature of Agile projects can sometimes lead to high-pressure environments where teams are expected to deliver frequent updates and improvements. Without proper support and balance, this can contribute to team member burnout.

10. **Resistance to Change**: Adopting an Agile approach requires a cultural shift within organizations accustomed to traditional methodologies – even a major paradigm shift for many. Resistance to change from stakeholders or team members can hinder the successful implementation of Agile practices.

To mitigate these potential downsides, Agile teams must emphasize clear communication, effective prioritization, stakeholder engagement, and continuous learning and adaptation throughout the project lifecycle. Tailoring Agile practices to fit the specific needs and context of the organization can also help in maximizing the benefits while minimizing the challenges.

3. Use Case Modeling:
- This methodology focuses on capturing and documenting requirements in the form of *use cases*, which describe interactions between users and the system.
- It helps in understanding how end-users will interact with the system and what specific functionalities are needed.

Risks of the Use Case Modeling

Use Case Modeling is a valuable technique for capturing and documenting requirements in a structured and user-centric manner. However, like any methodology, it has potential downsides and risks that teams should be aware of:

1. **Complexity in Large Systems**: Use Case Modeling may become cumbersome and complex when applied to very large or highly intricate systems. Managing a vast number of *use cases*, especially in systems with numerous *actors* (people, places, and things) and interactions, can lead to documentation overload and difficulty in maintaining clarity and coherence.

2. **Scope Creep**: Use Case modeling, if not managed carefully, can be susceptible to *scope creep*. As new use cases are identified or existing ones are expanded upon, there is a risk of expanding the scope of the project beyond its original boundaries. This can lead to increased development time and costs.

3. **Overemphasis on System Interactions**: Use Case Modeling primarily focuses on interactions between end-users (actors) and the system. This may result in less emphasis on non-functional requirements, such as performance, security, and scalability, which are equally critical for the success of the system. In my view, business requirements are best specified separately from system requirements. Use Case Modeling tends to focus on system interaction (implementation issues) rather than essential business requirements.

4. **Assumption of User Understanding**: Use Case Modeling assumes that stakeholders and end-users have a clear understanding of their requirements and interactions with the system. However, if stakeholders' understanding evolves or if there are misunderstandings during the initial stages, it can lead to inaccuracies or incomplete use case descriptions.

5. **Potential Rigidity**: Use Case Modeling typically follows a structured approach, which may not easily accommodate changes in requirements or evolving user needs during later stages of development. Use Cases tend to focus on existing system dialogues, and often struggle with new business requirements since the focus is on interactions rather than essential requirements. Agile methodologies, which allow for more flexibility and iterative adjustments, may be more suitable in such dynamic environments.

6. **Focus on Functional Requirements**: While Use Case Modeling is effective in capturing the interactions between actors and the system to deliver functional requirements, it may not fully address data requirements to meet the objectives of a business process. Teams may need to supplement Use Case Modeling with other techniques – like data modeling – to ensure comprehensive coverage of all project requirements. This often leads to specifications that are fragmented and not easily understood.

7. **Skill and Expertise Requirement**: Developing effective Use Case models requires skill and expertise in requirements elicitation, modeling techniques, and

understanding of end-user interactions. Inexperienced teams or those unfamiliar with the methodology may struggle to create meaningful and useful Use Cases.

To mitigate these potential downsides, teams using Use Case Modeling should emphasize clear communication, stakeholder involvement, and validation throughout the process. It's also sometimes necessary to combine Use Case Modeling with other methodologies or techniques as needed to ensure a holistic approach to requirements gathering and documentation.

4. **Joint Application Development (JAD) and Rapid Application Development (RAD)**:

- JAD and RAD are collaborative approaches where stakeholders, including end-users and developers, come together in a room for intensive workshops to define and clarify requirements.

- It encourages direct communication and can speed up the requirement gathering process.

- Both approaches encourage the use of technologies to rapidly capture requirements and prototype development wherever possible.

Risks of JAD and RAD

While Joint Application Development (JAD) and Rapid Application Development (RAD) offer significant benefits in terms of collaboration and efficiency in requirements gathering, there are also potential downsides and risks to consider, as identified below.

1. **Resource Intensive**: JAD and RAD sessions require the active participation of stakeholders, including end-users

and developers, for extended periods. This can be resource-intensive in terms of time commitment and availability, especially for stakeholders who have other responsibilities or are located in different geographical locations.

2. **Costly**: Conducting JAD or RAD sessions, especially multiple sessions throughout the project lifecycle, can be costly in terms of facilitation, logistics, and organizational resources. The expenses associated with organizing and managing these workshops need to be justified by the value derived from clearer requirements and reduced rework.

3. **Conflict Resolution Challenges**: In JAD and RAD sessions, stakeholders with different perspectives and priorities may come into conflict over requirements and their proposed solutions. Resolving these conflicts in real-time during the workshops can be challenging and will always require skilled facilitation to ensure productive outcomes.

4. **Time Constraints**: While JAD and RAD aim to expedite the requirement gathering process, the focus is almost always on solution development rather than business requirements. Also, there may be time constraints that limit the depth of discussions or the ability to thoroughly explore all potential requirements and scenarios. Rushed decision-making or incomplete exploration of requirements can lead to misunderstandings or incomplete documentation.

5. **Over-reliance on Workshop Dynamics**: The effectiveness of JAD and RAD heavily depends on the dynamics and interactions within the workshop sessions. If the sessions are not well-facilitated or if key stakeholders are not fully engaged, the quality and accuracy of the gathered requirements will be compromised. This is especially true when JAD/RAD sessions focus on solution delivery, which is almost always.

6. **Documentation Challenges**: Despite their collaborative nature, JAD/RAD sessions don't always result in complete documentation of requirements, as there is a perception (often a reality) that the documentation is reflected in the solution design. Accordingly, there may be a need for additional effort to translate workshop outcomes into comprehensive requirement specifications that can guide the development process effectively.

7. **Resistance to Change**: Adopting JAD/RAD may require a cultural shift within organizations that are accustomed to more conventional requirement gathering methods. Resistance to change from stakeholders or team members who prefer other approaches can impact the successful implementation of JAD/RAD practices.

To mitigate these potential downsides, organizations implementing JAD/RAD must invest in experienced and skilled facilitators, establish clear objectives and agendas for sessions, ensure adequate preparation and follow-up, and maintain open communication channels with stakeholders throughout the project lifecycle. Balancing the benefits of collaborative requirement gathering with the challenges involved is key to leveraging JAD/RAD effectively.

5. **Prototyping**:
   - In this methodology, prototypes or mock-ups of the system are created early in the project to visualize requirements.
   - Stakeholders can interact with these prototypes to provide feedback and refine their requirements.

Risks of Prototyping

Prototyping is a methodology that offers advantages in terms of early visualization, stakeholder engagement, and iterative refinement of requirements. However, there are several potential downsides and risks to consider when prototyping:

1. **Incomplete or Inaccurate Requirements**: Prototyping focuses on quickly creating a working model of the system software and interaction to gather feedback and refine requirements. If requirements are not well-understood or defined at the outset, there is a risk that the initial prototype may not accurately reflect all necessary functionalities or may omit critical features. Prototypes, by definition, are snapshots of pieces of software that make up the system. A fully integrated system is difficult – not impossible – to achieve using prototyping as a strategy. Business requirements are typically piecemeal, as is the resulting prototype, which still has to be developed to its fully integrated functionality.

2. **Scope Creep**: Stakeholder interaction with prototypes can lead to additional feature requests or changes that expand the scope of the project beyond its original boundaries. Without careful management, this scope creep can impact project timelines, budgets, and overall project success.

3. **Increased Development Time and Cost**: Prototyping – especially iterative prototyping – requires time and effort to create, test, and refine multiple versions of the prototype based on stakeholder feedback. This iterative process can lead to increased development costs and longer project timelines compared to more linear methodologies. Also, prototyping deals with the technical side of a project – the software. Software is seen as the solution. Prototyping does not address the essential business requirements outside software development, such as new business requirements and interactions.

4. **Potential for Miscommunication**: Stakeholders and development teams may interpret prototypes differently, leading to misunderstandings or discrepancies in requirements. Clear communication and documentation are essential to ensure that feedback from stakeholders is accurately translated into actionable requirements.

5. **Risk of Prototype Over-Engineering**: There is a possibility that prototypes may be over-engineered or developed to a level of complexity beyond what is needed for validation and feedback. This can result in

wasted effort and resources if significant changes are later required based on stakeholder feedback.

6. **Technical Debt**: Rapid prototyping may prioritize speed and quick feedback over long-term technical considerations such as scalability, maintainability, and performance. This can lead to the accumulation of technical debt if proper attention is not given to refining and aligning the prototype with architectural and technical requirements.

7. **Dependency on Prototype Quality**: The effectiveness of prototyping relies heavily on the quality and fidelity of the prototype itself. If prototypes are not representative of the final system or if they lack essential functionalities, stakeholders may provide feedback based on incomplete or inaccurate information.

To mitigate these potential downsides, prototyping projects should establish clear goals and objectives for prototyping activities, involve key stakeholders early and throughout the process, prioritize requirements validation and documentation, and carefully manage scope changes through iterative refinement and prioritization. Balancing the benefits of rapid feedback and visualization with the challenges involved in prototyping is crucial for successful project outcomes.

Also, since prototypes typically only address the software component of a project, project management must take action to complete other new or enhanced business requirements that are not inside the boundaries of software development.

6. **Requirements Workshops**:
   - These are facilitated sessions where stakeholders discuss and document their requirements collectively.
   - Workshops can be effective in resolving conflicts and ensuring a shared understanding of requirements.

Risks of Requirements Workshops

While requirements workshops offer many benefits in terms of collaboration, clarity, and stakeholder engagement, they also come with potential downsides that should be considered.

1. **Time-Consuming**: Requirements workshops require the active participation of stakeholders for extended periods of time. This can be demanding on their schedules, especially for stakeholders with other responsibilities or when participants are located in different time zones. Stakeholders do have their own regular jobs.

2. **Costs**: Organizing and facilitating requirements workshops can be costly, particularly if they involve travel, accommodation, or specialized facilitation services. The expenses associated with conducting workshops need to be justified by the value derived from clearer requirements and reduced rework. It is difficult to conduct requirements workshops via Zoom or Teams.

3. **Dominance of Strong Personalities**: In workshops, stakeholders with strong personalities or seniority within the organization may dominate discussions. This can lead

to less input from quieter stakeholders or those with differing perspectives, potentially resulting in incomplete or biased requirements.

4. **Groupthink**: There is a risk of groupthink in requirements workshops, where participants conform to the opinions or decisions of the majority without critically evaluating alternatives. This can limit creativity and lead to overlooked requirements or suboptimal solutions.

5. **Lack of Follow-Up**: If decisions or agreements made during workshops are not documented or followed up effectively, there may be misunderstandings or discrepancies in requirements later in the project lifecycle. Clear documentation and communication of workshop outcomes are essential for maintaining alignment and accountability.

6. **Skill and Facilitation Challenges**: Effective facilitation is critical to the success of requirements workshops. Inexperienced or ineffective facilitators may struggle to manage group dynamics, guide discussions, and ensure different viewpoints are heard and considered. Skillful facilitation requires training and experience. The lack of skill (and even knowledge) by facilitators – who should be senior analysts – is much more common than not. This is a significant challenge for many organizations.

7. **Dependency on Workshop Dynamics**: The success of requirements workshops depends heavily on the dynamics and interactions among participants. If workshops are not well-planned or if there are

interpersonal conflicts or misunderstandings, the quality and accuracy of the requirements gathered may be compromised. Once again, this comes down to the skill and knowledge of the facilitator (the analyst). Workshop dynamics do not happen on their own, nor can it happen when a session is led by an inexperienced – or even junior – analyst.

8. **Limited Remote Participation**: In distributed or global teams, organizing face-to-face requirements workshops may be impractical or costly. Virtual workshops can be challenging to facilitate effectively, especially when dealing with cultural or language differences. Virtual Zoom or Teams sessions are particularly difficult for workshops that require a high level of visibility. It can be done, but requires excellent skills and ability to use the technology effectively.

To mitigate these potential risks and downsides, organizations must carefully plan and prepare for requirements workshops, ensuring diverse representation of stakeholders, clear objectives, skilled facilitation, and follow-up mechanisms to validate and document workshop outcomes. Balancing the benefits of collaborative requirements gathering with the challenges involved in workshop dynamics is key to maximizing the effectiveness of requirements workshops.

7. **Interviews and Surveys**:
   - Direct interviews with stakeholders and the use of surveys can be helpful in gathering specific and targeted information about requirements.
   - They are often used in combination with other methodologies.

Downsides and Extreme Risks of Stakeholder Interviews

While stakeholder interviews are a valuable tool for gathering specific and targeted information about project requirements, they come with several potential downsides.

1. Bias and Subjectivity

Personal Biases: Stakeholders may present information that is influenced by their personal opinions, experiences, and interests, rather than objective facts. Interviews tend to be variable in nature (everyone is different) and seldom focused on business rules in a specific process or situational context.

Selective Reporting: Some stakeholders might emphasize certain aspects of the project while downplaying others, leading to a skewed understanding of requirements. Prioritization of requirements is often based on the preference of the most senior person at the expense of the most knowledgeable.

2. Incomplete Information

Limited Scope: Individual stakeholders may only provide insights related to their specific role or perspective, resulting in a fragmented view of the project requirements. Individual stakeholders generally see their area of responsibility as the center of the universe; therefore, they sometimes emphasize the critical nature and importance of their perspective. This can influence the analyst.

Overlooked Details: Important requirements might be missed if stakeholders are not fully aware of all the aspects of the project or the needs of other stakeholders. In business or system requirements that span several different areas of responsibility, this is quite common.

3. Communication Barriers
Misunderstandings: Misinterpretations can occur if stakeholders and interviewers do not share a common understanding of terminology or project goals. Misinterpretation can also occur simply because the business language of one unit (or individual) may not be common with others. Meanings of terms can and often do vary.

Language and Cultural Differences: These can further complicate communication, especially in diverse or international teams. Business practices may differ, leading to assumptions of understanding that are simply incorrect.

4. Time-Consuming
Scheduling Conflicts: Coordinating interviews with busy stakeholders can be challenging and time-consuming. The larger the pool of stakeholders, the more complex scheduling gets and the longer it takes.

Lengthy Process: Conducting, documenting, and analyzing interviews can take a considerable amount of time, potentially delaying the project timeline. Interviews for business system requirements cannot be accurately done, in my opinion, by interviewing a "smaller representative group of stakeholders". This is almost guaranteed to miss a lot of important information. Building an expensive system cannot be based on "close counts". To conduct a full set of interviews – to gather the requirements correctly – you must pair each person interviewed with each of all the others to be interviewed: known as the *combination formula* or *binomial coefficient*. So, if you have 10 stakeholders, you will need to interview each with every other stakeholder, which results in 45 interviews. It is not uncommon that a complex system has 30 or more stakeholders. That would result in 435 interviews if no one is skipped. This is not reasonable. But neither is a "representative group of stakeholders".

5. **Inconsistencies**

Varied Responses: Different stakeholders may provide conflicting information, making it difficult to reconcile discrepancies and reach a consensus. Imagine the complexities created with this scenario when there are 10, 20, or 30 stakeholders with perspectives. And what happens when they are spread across the country, or even in different countries?

Changing Requirements: Stakeholders' requirements and priorities may evolve over time, leading to inconsistencies in the gathered information. Often, new business requirements are discovered after discussing known requirements. This can lead to even more changes. As I mentioned earlier, business requirements analysis is recursive in nature, which is a concept not supported by stakeholder interviews.

6. Dependence on Interviewer Skills

<u>Interviewer Expertise</u>: The quality of information gathered is heavily dependent on the interviewer's ability to ask the right questions and probe effectively. Many larger consulting firms use generic lists of questions to probe for business requirements. This discourages creative dialogue and the pursuit of **new** business requirements. It can also easily be done – even better – by generative artificial intelligence (AI). These generic industry-specific lists of questions are doomed to be replaced by AI, which is becoming more effective in the requirements analysis space every day.

<u>Bias in Interviewing</u>: Interviewers may inadvertently introduce their own biases into the conversation, affecting the responses they elicit. This is quite common. It's usually based on the interviewer's education and experience, and how they structure their questions.

7. Limited Scope for Follow-up

<u>Static Data</u>: Once a series of interviews are concluded, it might be difficult to go back for additional clarification or follow-up questions without further disrupting the stakeholders' schedules. Some analysts think stakeholders should be available to them at any time, all the time. Stakeholders have their own work to do. And since interviews can take a very long time, whatever information that's gathered is probably a snapshot in

time, and may not be representative of a new (and future) business system.

Documentation Challenges: Ensuring that all the information is accurately recorded and interpreted correctly can be challenging. Multiple interviews generally result in copious written documentation, often leading to stakeholders not doing the reading (and modifications) they should. Getting approval or sign-off from stakeholders is notoriously challenging in most organization. And, in many cases, to avoid confrontation and more time-consuming work, key stakeholders often begrudgingly sign-off (if there is such a process) without fully reviewing the requirements, while they hold their noses.

8. **Document Analysis**:
   - Analyzing existing documents, such as business processes, reports, and user manuals, can provide insights into current requirements and areas for improvement.

Downsides and Risks of Document Analysis

Document analysis is seen by some as a valuable technique for gathering requirements by examining existing documents such as business processes, reports, and user manuals. However, it also comes with potential downsides that should be considered:

1. **Incomplete or Outdated Information**: Documents usually do not provide a comprehensive or up-to-date view of the current state of requirements. They may lack details on recent changes, evolving business needs, or

undocumented practices that are critical to understanding the full scope of requirements.

2. **Assumptions and Interpretations**: Analyzing documents relies on interpreting and synthesizing information from various sources. Different analysts may interpret the same document differently, leading to discrepancies or misunderstandings in requirements.

3. **Limited Stakeholder Involvement**: Document analysis typically does not involve direct interaction with stakeholders. This can result in a lack of clarity or depth in understanding stakeholder perspectives, priorities, and underlying reasons for certain requirements.

4. **Difficulty in Identifying Implicit Requirements**: Documents will likely not state all requirements, especially those that are new, implicit, or assumed. Identifying these hidden requirements often requires additional context or clarification that are usually not evident from document analysis alone.

5. **Lack of Contextual Understanding**: Documents typically do not provide the full context or background information necessary to fully understand requirements. This can lead to misinterpretations or incomplete insights into the motivations behind certain requirements.

6. **Dependency on Document Quality**: The effectiveness of document analysis depends heavily on the quality, accuracy, and completeness of the documents being analyzed. Poorly maintained or inconsistent

documentation (which is the norm) can hinder the reliability of the requirements derived from this technique. Often, for large and mature business systems, there simply is no documentation that can be trusted.

7. **Limited Exploration of Alternatives**: Document analysis focuses on existing processes and requirements rather than exploring new, innovative, or alternative solutions. This can restrict opportunities for improvement or innovation in the project.

To mitigate these potential downsides, organizations should complement document analysis with other requirement gathering techniques. Cross-verifying information from multiple sources and involving stakeholders in validating and refining requirements are also essential practices to ensure comprehensive and accurate requirement documentation.

9. **Requirements Traceability**:
   - This approach involves mapping requirements to business objectives and ensuring that each requirement can be traced back to a specific need or goal.

Downsides and Risks of Requirements Traceability

While requirements traceability offers significant benefits in terms of clarity, alignment, and accountability in projects, there are potential downsides that should be considered:

1. **Overhead and Complexity**: Maintaining traceability matrices or tracking systems will introduce additional

overhead and complexity to the project management process. This includes the effort required to establish traceability links, update them as requirements evolve, and ensure consistency across different project artifacts.

2. **Resource Intensive**: Establishing and maintaining requirements traceability requires time, effort, and resources from project stakeholders, analysts, and project managers. This can be particularly challenging in projects with tight timelines or limited resources.

3. **Potential for Over-Engineering**: Focusing too heavily on traceability may lead to over-engineering or excessive documentation, where the effort to maintain traceability links outweighs the actual benefits gained. This can divert resources from more critical project activities, leading to project scheduling and budget challenges.

4. **Complexity in Change Management**: While traceability helps in understanding the impact of changes on requirements, managing changes across interconnected requirements and project artifacts can become complex. This complexity increases as the project progresses and requirements evolve.

5. **Risk of Misinterpretation**: Establishing traceability links requires clear understanding and interpretation of both business objectives and requirements. Misinterpretations or incorrect mappings can lead to traceability links that do not accurately reflect the true relationship between requirements and business goals.

6. **Dependency on Tooling**: Traceability often relies on specialized tools or software to manage and track relationships between requirements, business objectives, and other project artifacts. Dependency on these tools can introduce risks related to tool compatibility, support, and maintenance.

7. **Focus on Compliance Rather than Value**: In some cases, traceability may prioritize compliance with project management standards or regulations over delivering value to stakeholders. This can result in bureaucratic overhead and a lack of focus on achieving project objectives efficiently. This is counter to an agile philosophy and good business results.

To mitigate these potential downsides, organizations should adopt a balanced approach to requirements traceability that aligns with project goals and priorities. This includes focusing on traceability links that provide meaningful insights into project progress and alignment with business objectives, while avoiding unnecessary complexity and overhead. Regular reviews, and clear communication are crucial to ensuring that traceability efforts contribute positively to project outcomes.

The choice of methodology depends on the project's nature, size, complexity, and the organization's culture. In practice, many projects may use a combination of these methodologies or adapt them to suit their specific needs. The key is to select an approach that facilitates effective communication, collaboration, and the accurate capture of business system requirements to ensure project success.

The Pitfalls of Conventional Analysis Methods and Management

> *"The illiterate of the 21st century will not be those who cannot read and write, but those who cannot learn, unlearn, and relearn."*
> – Alvin Toffler –
> Alvin Toffler was an American writer, futurist, and businessman known for his works discussing modern technologies, including the digital revolution and the communication revolution, with emphasis on their effects on cultures worldwide.

Many of the preceding analysis methodologies are conventional and widely used. Some have been around for several decades. Some of them, although developed with the best of intentions, have little value today to offer business system analysts or project managers. With some of these methodologies, it is nearly impossible to uncover all business requirements. This leads to telling stakeholders *"you didn't tell me"* and stakeholders saying, *"you didn't ask"* when we get to testing time. It's a problem almost very organization has now, and has had since the beginning of time. Incomplete requirements is by far the biggest issue, not so much inaccurate requirements.

Analysts usually do a good job with the tools they have. Their tools are the methodologies they use, or those which are sometimes imposed on them.

Conventional analysis methodologies range from really awful to pretty good. So, going forward – you get to decide what's in the "pretty good" category. These include most methods that fall under the structured analysis, object-oriented analysis, and data modeling schools of thought. Unfortunately, almost all of the conventional analysis methodologies listed earlier have similar problems.

Client expectations are hard to manage.
Business system analysts are expected to know all about their client's business – what it is, how it works, and all the finite details. The analyst is also expected to have all the solutions to the problems, whether these have been identified or not. This appears to include reading the client's mind about the future.

Analysts need more time to become intimately familiar with the client's business.
There is general agreement by corporate management that the analyst needs to become familiar with the details of the client's business when a project first starts. But, the time needed to ramp up is almost always perceived to delay the project and increase costs.

This contradiction creates conflict, so many managers simply reduce the amount of time budgeted for business requirements analysis. The resulting lack of time to properly understand the client's business often leads to the necessary risk of approximating the true requirements. Also, the resulting lack of time to ramp up often results in a system that doesn't address all the client's requirements.

The client is often disappointed with the results, stating one of the following reasons:
1) Since the client usually perceives that the team will create the business requirements as part of the technical solution, there is an expectation that

knowing the technical solution also means completely understanding the business requirements – an analyst's paradox.

2) The time from business requirements to solution delivery is too long, and the installed system no longer meets the client's current business needs.

3) The system does what the client asked for, but not what was needed. It was expected that a professional business analyst would bridge that gap.

4) The business requirement specification was not clear, leading to ambiguity and problems down the line, especially during testing.

5) The system has to be revised over and over again, before the client accepts it.

All of these challenges can be mitigated or even eliminated by two factors: (1) using an analysis methodology that's proven to deliver a complete and accurate requirements specification (check what you mean by "proven"); and (2) a project management approach that is focused on the specifics of business system analysis rather than general project management.

Before going on the that specific project management approach, let's look at the professional's success code, as I see it.

The Professional's Project Success Code

> *"Get the right people. Then no matter what else you might do wrong after that, the people will save you. That's what management is all about."*
> – Tom DeMarco –

Tom DeMarco is an American software development expert, author, and consultant on software engineering subjects. Tom was awarded a Warnier Prize for lifetime contributions to the field of computing, and Stevens Award for contributions to the methods of software development.

To be successful on the projects we take on we must not only have a good system acquisition methodology – one that supports agility and responsiveness without chaos and risk – we must have an agile approach to business requirements analysis that is predictable and repeatable as well. What I mean by this is that every analyst who applies the methodology should apply it more or less the same way. It also means that if different analysts do the same work, the result should be the same too. If the result is the same, then the methodology has a strong scientific foundation, rather than results being based on best efforts by the most available person.

Every professional must have a foundation that guides all system acquisition or development work. I believe the foundation can be best described as follows:

- **Be on budget, on time, no problems.**

The project manager or team leader must be committed to ensuring that the project is problem-free, on budget, and all deadlines are met. Since what is done up front determines all subsequent results, the approach to business system analysis you use on your project must make this objective possible.

- **Foster teamwork and client participation.**

The best relationship you can have with your stakeholders is one of partnership, teamwork and active participation. The best results come when you work directly and visibly with your stakeholders. Never work in isolation from them. This approach to business system analysis helps make the partnership possible.

- **Apply hands-on modern management methods.**
- **Encourage on-project coaching and mentoring.**
- **Get management commitment to the project.**

Every project should be guided directly by a practicing expert in the tools, techniques and methodologies to be used on the project. It's a lot easier to advance when everyone is on board and understands how the work is actually done, rather than relying on theory passed on from an absentee practitioner or methodologist.

Management commitment and sponsorship is also enormously necessary to a project's success, as is a well-defined and developed professional development program for the business analysts and system developers. This approach to business system analysis helps to make all of this possible.

- **Be highly visible.**

My experience is that an informed and involved client will usually make the best decisions. We have found that visibility – contrary to popular myth – eliminates fear, uncertainty and doubt by the business community. Visibility always results in interaction and ownership. Don't hide from sight or work in isolation from the client. Have pride in your work. Success is the only option. The nature of the "discovery" sessions you use to uncover the full set of business system requirements must help to make this possible.

- **Use best practices.**

Always use the best and most modern methods. This always results in faster results, less money being spent, and the highest quality. Always look for better ways. Avoid the 'Not Invented Here (NIH)' syndrome. Look outside your organization. Be devoted to finding the best methods available. And then measure satisfaction by your client community.

- **Apply the best methodologies.**

Use the most effective and pragmatic methodologies that you can find. Don't use them because they are popular, or the *solution du jour*; use them because they have an excellent track-record according to your clients and subject-matter experts. While I naturally suggest you apply the event-based business system analysis approach I've described in my other books, on big or small projects, adapt it as required to your organization, your industry, and your personal style of working. This will help you get the best results.

- **Use common sense – and a coach and mentor.**

A popular old saying is, *"common sense just isn't very common."* But I think it is. The first step is to get yourself a personal business analysis coach and mentor, and ask that person for some help whenever it's needed. Take a practical, common-sense approach to all projects. Every situation is unique, and each has different needs. Make sure your approach to project work supports this.

Book II

The 5-Point Project Plan

The 5-Point Project Plan

"If you don't know where you're going, you'll end up someplace else."
– Yogi Berra –
American baseball player, manager, and coach.

This 5-point project plan is designed to be specific to the front-end business requirements analysis of a project. The following is an overview of the objectives and resulting artifacts (deliverables). After the overview, I'll expand with more details upon the work required, project management aspects, and the deliverables.

Any plan to uncover and specify business system requirements must be <u>specific</u> and <u>measurable</u>, not just another item on the list to be checked off. A plan must clearly identify what's to be done, by whom, and when. It must specify accurately the time and schedule involved. And it must be measurable – or it's just more of the Same Old Stuff made up of guesswork, magic numbers and unicorns.

1. **Initiate & Plan.** Working with your client …

    - Identify the "pilots" and "co-pilots" for the project. If you are the senior analyst on the project, then you're the "pilot".

    - Assignments include analyzing and documenting the project rationale, mandate, perceived scope, stakeholders, subject-matter experts, discovery session schedules, identified risks, expectations, and budget for the project.

- You'll also want to define the metrics required to measure project "success", and the acceptance approval process for the business requirements.

- Also, create a detailed list and definition of the deliverables and artifacts expected from the business requirements segment of the project.

Outcome: Business Analysis Plan

2. Conduct Project Scope Blitz.

- Even if your client believes they have the scope all figured out, you will still need to conduct a *Project Scope Blitz* for stakeholders and SMEs.

- This will require a ½-day or a full day. This highly interactive discovery session identifies the conditions and circumstances the business must deal with (for your project), at a workable *business event* level, as well as the business areas and departments involved at each stage of business analysis. It delivers a high-level, initial *Project Business Event List*. This enables you to schedule detailed discovery sessions. It also sets the tone for the project, right up front, and establishes your credibility as a business analyst.

Outcome: Project Business Event List

3. Plan Detailed Discovery Sessions.

- Based on the *Project Business Event List*, create a schedule for each detailed discovery session and the subject-matter experts (SMEs) that are required to participate. Also, define the exact amount of time required to complete the project's business requirements analysis. (The metric we use in our organization is: 4 hours per *business event*, consisting of a 1-hour discovery session with stakeholders and 3 hours to complete the analysis and documentation.)

- The resulting schedule is highly dynamic, based on your SMEs' availability and other priorities by the client. However, deadlines can be set at this time.

Outcome: Project Discovery Schedule

4. Conduct Detailed Discovery Sessions.

- Based on the *Project Discovery Schedule*, invite the identified subject-matter experts (SMEs) and conduct interactive one-hour discovery sessions for each *business event* to complete the business requirements for the project.

- Complete the remaining documentation for each *business event*.

Outcome: Project Business Requirements

5. Coordinate Business Analysis Completion.

- Depending on your mandate, you – as the business analyst and "pilot" for the project – will coordinate completion of the business analysis part of the project. The project may be phased or staged, which usually means you will "pilot" each stage of business analysis.

- It will almost certainly extend into the solution design or software acquisition stage. If this is the case, it would be most productive if you were part of the team guiding the technology team through the business requirements.

- Lessons learned from all the discovery sessions are also integrated and documented now.

Outcome: Business Analysis Project Review

There is absolutely no need to make this more complicated than it is. The objective of front-end requirements analysis is to deliver value as quickly as possible to the client.

Applying the principle of *"partition the effort to minimize complexity"* (the first principle of analysis), let's address each of the five points in the business requirements analysis project plan.

1. **Initiate & Plan.** Working with your client ...
   - Identify the "pilots" and "co-pilots" for the project. If you are the senior analyst on the project, then you're the "pilot".

   - Assignments include analyzing and documenting the project rationale, mandate, perceived scope, stakeholders, subject-matter experts, discovery session schedules, identified risks, expectations, and budget for the project.

   - You'll also want to define the metrics required to measure project "success", and the acceptance approval process for the business requirements.

   - Also, create a detailed list and definition of the deliverables and artifacts expected from the business requirements segment of the project.

   Outcome: <u>Business Analysis Plan</u>

The first step of initiating and planning sets the foundation for the entire project. It involves identifying key roles, such as the project "pilot" and "co-pilot," and outlining the project's scope, stakeholders, risks, and budget.

Identifying Key Roles

The success of any project heavily relies on the clarity of roles and responsibilities. The "pilot" role is similar to that of a project manager, but with a stronger emphasis on aligning the front-end requirements analysis project with the business's strategic goals.

The roles of the project "pilot" and "co-pilot" are critical for steering the front-end of the project in the right direction. The senior analyst usually takes on the role of "pilot," guiding the business requirements project to ensure it aligns with business objectives. This person is responsible for the overall direction of the front-end of the project, ensuring that all aspects are coordinated and aligned with the business goals. The "pilot" requires a deep understanding of the project's objectives. They must also have the ability to communicate effectively with both the project team and stakeholders. This role involves strategic thinking, decision-making, and a comprehensive understanding of business processes and requirements.

Effective communication skills are vital, as the pilot will be the main point of contact for all stakeholders, ensuring their expectations are managed and their inputs are integrated into the project plan.

The "co-pilot" is equally important, but different. This person typically assists in managing tasks and communications. In discovery sessions they capture business rules, narratives, business objects, data items, and any notes required. This role supports the "pilot" by managing operational aspects of the project, coordinating meetings (discovery sessions), and ensuring that all team members are aware of their responsibilities and deadlines. The co-pilot must be detail-oriented, organized, and possess excellent communication skills to manage the project's logistical aspects efficiently.

Defining Assignments

Defining assignments is a crucial first step in any requirements analysis project. It involves analyzing and documenting the project rationale, mandate, and perceived scope. I say "perceived scope" because most projects start with a mandate from on-high rather than an actual analysis of what's required to meet the business objectives. While sometimes there are detailed feasibility studies, often there are not. We'll deal with the real scope – still meeting the mandate – a little later.

The project rationale explains why the project is necessary and what it aims to achieve. This involves understanding the business challenge or opportunity that the project addresses and articulating this in a way that all stakeholders can understand. The initial mandate also outlines the authority and responsibility of the project team, setting clear boundaries for what the project will and will not address.

Identifying stakeholders and subject-matter experts (SMEs) is crucial because they provide the insights and information needed to define the requirements of the project. Stakeholders are those who have an interest in the project, either because they are directly affected by it or because they have the authority to influence its outcome. SMEs, on the other hand, are those with specialized knowledge that is critical to the project. Engaging these individuals early in the project ensures that their needs and expectations are understood and considered.

Scheduling *discovery sessions* (we'll address discovery sessions later) with these stakeholders and SMEs is the next step. These sessions are opportunities to gather detailed information about their needs, expectations, and constraints, always within a specific context rather than general requirements. Each discovery session is a forum for "discovery" or uncovering of specific, detailed business requirements – addressing process and data –

and a place for discussion and collaboration, ensuring that different perspectives are considered.

Recognizing potential risks is another critical component. It involves identifying any factors that could hinder the project's progress or success. These risks could be internal and include resource limitations, technological challenges, or conflicting stakeholder interests. Risks could also be external, such as changes in market conditions or regulatory requirements. By identifying these risks early, the project team can develop strategies to mitigate them.

Defining expectations and budget constraints involves setting realistic goals for what the project aims to achieve and outlining the financial resources available. This process requires a careful balance between what is desirable and what is feasible. Determination of feasibility is, however, usually tied to available or affordable technology, or social desirability of specific processes or data.

Clear documentation of each assignment, specifying the tasks to be completed, the responsible parties, and the deadlines, serves as a reference throughout the project, ensuring that everyone is aware of their roles and responsibilities. It helps prevent misunderstandings and ensures that all aspects of the project are covered.

Setting Metrics for Success
Defining metrics for success is crucial for evaluating the project's progress and outcomes. These metrics should be specific, measurable, achievable, relevant, and time-bound (SMART). Examples of metrics include the

completion of project milestones on time, staying within budget, and meeting the defined quality standards.

I'm a strong supporter of the idea that we can measure anything that exists. Even so-called soft benefits. This means we can have a metric for anything to be done or delivered on a project. The real issue about most metrics is their contextual relevance. While it's important that we measure – so that we can estimate – the process of measurement should not become a mindless method of judgement based on metrics.

Projects need to have an acceptance process – one that actually works. This includes an acceptance approval process for the project's business requirements. This involves setting criteria for determining whether the requirements are (a) complete (we know we got them all), and (b) accurate (we know we got the right ones).

For example, if one of the business objectives of the project is to improve business processes, metrics might include the time saved, the reduction in errors, or the increase in customer satisfaction. Each of these must be measurable. These metrics provide a tangible way to measure the project's impact and ensure that it delivers the expected benefits.

Metrics should include:

- Timeline Adherence: Monitoring whether project milestones are met according to the schedule.

- Budget Compliance: Ensuring that the project stays within the allocated budget.

- Quality Standards: Measuring whether the project deliverables meet the predefined quality criteria.

- <u>Stakeholder Satisfaction</u>: Assessing the satisfaction levels of stakeholders and their engagement throughout the project.

Regularly reviewing these metrics helps in maintaining the project's momentum and making necessary adjustments to address any issues that arise. This ongoing review process ensures that the project remains aligned with its objectives and that deviations are quickly identified and corrected.

Listing Deliverables and Artifacts

Creating a detailed list of deliverables and artifacts expected from the business requirements part of the project ensures that all necessary components are accounted for, and nothing is overlooked. Deliverables may include project plans, business requirements specifications, technology notes, and initial training plans. Each deliverable should have a clear description, including its purpose, content, and due date. This list should be reviewed and updated regularly throughout the project to ensure that all necessary documents are created and delivered on time.

Deliverables should include:

- **Project Plans:**
  Detailed plans outlining the project's scope, objectives, timeline, and resources. It provides a roadmap for the project, ensuring that all team members understand their roles and responsibilities and how their work contributes to the overall project goals. It includes a list of Project Events derived from the front-end Scope Blitz. (Business Events are

conditions, circumstances, and situations the target system has to respond to.)

- **Business Requirements Specification:**
  This specification captures and describes all the business requirements in detail. It serves as a reference throughout the ongoing project, ensuring that all stakeholders are aware of the requirements and how they will be addressed. This specification must be detailed and specific, providing a clear and comprehensive description of the business needs and expectations. It includes all Business Processes, Business Objects, contextual Business Rules, required Business Data, and descriptive Narratives.

- **Technology Notes:**
  The Business Requirements Specification should be fundamentally free of implementation technologies. Front-end requirements analysis should never be about **how** something is implemented (the technology), but rather about **what data and functionality** is required to meet business needs, without the volatility of technology choices or changes. But you and I know that literally every project starts with a mandate to apply certain technologies. Almost all projects have a dictated technology bias from the very start. This means it will be impossible to ignore certain implementation issues as we uncover more of the business requirements. But it shouldn't mean that the business will be designed around the technology. The business requirements should still be analyzed independently of the tech to be applied. What this really means, is that we can take technology notes as we go along. Keep the tech notes separate from the essential business requirements, but without ignoring them. It's important to keep a separate repository of

tech notes, each in context of specific business situations or circumstances (*events*), and to not embed them into the actual business requirement. This independence of the business requirement, while recognizing the technology and possible implementation, still allows the flexibility of assessing other (perhaps innovative) tech solutions as the project progresses.

- **Initial Training Plans:**
Front-end business requirements analysis is not responsible for the detailed training plans that may be necessary after the system is designed and implemented. However, front-end analysis will always recognize new or modified areas of the business system, whether executed by software or without. These new areas can all be identified as needing end-user training, without getting into the specifics of a training program. This could include clients or actors external to the "system" that may need guidance in using the "system".

Regularly reviewing and possibly updating the list of deliverables ensures that the project stays on track and that all necessary specification data are prepared and delivered on time. This ongoing review process ensures that any changes in the project are reflected in the deliverables, maintaining their relevance and accuracy.

Outcome: Business Analysis Plan

The result of this phase is a comprehensive Business Analysis Plan that serves as a roadmap for the project. The Business Analysis Plan outlines all aspects of the project, including the objectives, scope, stakeholders, deliverables, schedule, and budget. It also includes a risk management plan, communication plan, and quality management plan. This document serves as a reference throughout the project, ensuring that all team members and stakeholders are aware of the project's goals and how they will be achieved.

The Business Analysis Plan will always include:

- Project Objectives: Clear and concise statements of what the project aims to achieve.

- Scope Definition: A detailed description of the project's boundaries and deliverables. At the very least, this should include a list of Business Events discovered through the Scope Blitz (more on this later).

- Stakeholder Identification: A list of all stakeholders and their roles and responsibilities.

- Deliverables List: A comprehensive list of all project deliverables and artifacts.

- Schedule and Timeline: A detailed timeline of the project, including all milestones and deadlines.

- Budget: An outline of the project's budget, including cost estimates for all activities.

- Risk Management Plan: A plan for identifying, assessing, and mitigating project risks.

- Communication Plan: A plan for how communication will be managed throughout the project.

- Quality Management Plan: A plan for ensuring that all project deliverables meet the required quality standards.

The Business Analysis Plan serves as the key reference throughout the project, from which team members and stakeholders will take their lead. Can it change as the front-end analysis progresses? Yes, most certainly. A Plan should not be etched in stone, although I have encountered some projects like that. It needs to be as living and dynamic as the business it supports is intended to be. So, if it needs change, enhancement, or updating of any kind – do it.

---

2. Conduct Project Scope Blitz.

- Even if your client believes they have the scope all figured out, you will still need to conduct a *Project Scope Blitz* for stakeholders and SMEs.

- This will require a ½-day or a full day. This highly interactive discovery session identifies the <u>conditions</u> and <u>circumstances</u> the business must deal with (for your project), at a workable *business event* level, as well as the business areas and departments involved at each stage of business analysis. It delivers a high-level, initial *Project Business Event List*. This enables you to schedule detailed discovery sessions. It also sets the tone for the project, right up front, and establishes your credibility as a business analyst.

Outcome: <u>Project Business Event List</u>

Despite any preconceived notions of the project scope, conducting a Project Scope Blitz with stakeholders and SMEs is essential.

Organizing the Scope Blitz

A Scope Blitz session can range from a half-day to a full day and is designed to be highly interactive. It aims to identify the conditions and circumstances the enhanced or the new business component must handle, by providing a list of business events that identify those conditions and circumstances. All project stakeholders, sponsors, and subject-matter experts are invited and should participate. This often makes for a room with many people, but it also ensures that every area is represented with subject-matter experts. It also gives stakeholders an opportunity to ask lots of questions, and to show support and ownership.

The agenda is very simple –

1. *To determine and itemize the individual business events – business conditions, situations, and circumstances – that are to be part of the project, and require either decomposition or expansion.*

2. *To determine the SMEs who need to participate in the individual interactive discovery sessions.*

3. *To accurately estimate duration of the full requirements analysis, to enable the scheduling of the discovery sessions."*

It isn't necessary to make the agenda any more complicated than this. The objective is to get everyone together, to get the Scope Blitz session started, and to arrive at a full set of objectives based on business events.

Engaging Stakeholders and SMEs

The project Scope Blitz brings together various business areas and departments who are involved in the project.

This first-day collaboration, when everyone is brought together (including by video for those who are remote), helps to create a high-level, initial Project Business Event List, which guides the scheduling of detailed discovery sessions. Engaging stakeholders and SMEs at this point is crucial to ensure that all relevant perspectives are considered and that the project addresses all necessary business situations and circumstances. This collaboration also helps to build buy-in and support for the project, ensuring that all stakeholders are committed to its success.

Creating the Project Business Event List

The primary outcome of the Scope Blitz is the Project Business Event List. This list outlines the major business events that the project will address, providing a high-level overview of the project's scope. This list serves as a foundation for the detailed discovery sessions, ensuring that all necessary business situations and circumstances are covered.

Setting the Tone for the Project

Conducting a successful Scope Blitz sets a positive tone for the project, demonstrating the lead business analyst's competence and establishing credibility with stakeholders. It also helps to build a sense of collaboration and shared purpose among the project team and SMEs. This positive tone can help to build momentum and ensure that the project progresses smoothly. The successful execution of the Scope Blitz demonstrates the competency and credibility of the project team, particularly the business analyst leading the session. By guiding productive discussions, synthesizing diverse viewpoints, and delivering actionable insights, a lead Business Analyst can establish themself as a trusted advisor and leader within the organization.

SMEs possess specialized knowledge and expertise in specific business areas or domains. Their participation in the Scope Blitz provides valuable insights into existing processes, challenges, and especially opportunities. SMEs help to validate business events, identify dependencies, and propose feasible alternatives. Yes, the vast majority of them know their business very well indeed.

A positive and engaging Scope Blitz sets the stage for future project activities, generating momentum and enthusiasm among stakeholders and team members. By showcasing early wins, addressing concerns proactively, and soliciting input from participants, project teams create a sense of optimism and confidence in the project's potential for success.

Outcome: Project Business Event List

The Project Business Event List serves as a foundation for the subsequent phases of the project, guiding the detailed discovery sessions. This list provides a clear and comprehensive overview of the business events (situations, conditions, and circumstances) that the project will address, ensuring that all necessary areas are covered.

Guiding Subsequent Activities

The Project Business Event List serves as a foundational artifact for the project, guiding subsequent activities such as detailed requirements gathering in discovery sessions, solution design, and implementation planning. It provides a common understanding of the project scope, objectives, and priorities, ensuring that all project stakeholders are aligned and focused on achieving the desired outcomes.

Supporting Decision-Making

Throughout the project, the Project Business Event List serves as a reference point for decision-making and prioritization. It helps project teams assess the impact of proposed changes, evaluate alternative solutions, and make informed trade-off decisions. By linking business events to organizational goals and objectives, project teams can justify investments and allocate resources effectively.

Facilitating Communication and Collaboration

The Project Business Event List facilitates communication and collaboration among project stakeholders and team members. It provides a shared language and framework for discussing project scope, requirements, and deliverables. By identifying business events, project teams can ensure clarity, consistency, and alignment across all project activities.

Conducting a Project Scope Blitz is a critical step in the project initiation phase. It brings together stakeholders and SMEs to collaboratively define the project scope, objectives, and boundaries. By identifying and prioritizing key business events, the Scope Blitz sets the stage for subsequent project activities and ensures alignment with organizational goals and stakeholder expectations. Through effective planning, facilitation, and stakeholder engagement, project teams can create a clear roadmap for project success and build momentum for achieving desired outcomes. The Project Business

Managing Successful Requirements Projects

Event List serves as a foundational artifact that guides decision-making, supports communication, and fosters collaboration throughout the project lifecycle. By leveraging the insights generated during the Scope Blitz, project teams can mitigate risks, maximize value delivery, and drive business transformation effectively.

3. **Plan Detailed Discovery Sessions.**

   - Based on the *Project Business Event List*, create a schedule for each detailed discovery session and the subject-matter experts (SMEs) that are required to participate. Also, define the exact amount of time required to complete the project's business requirements analysis. (The metric we use in our organization is: 4 hours per *business event*, consisting of a 1-hour discovery session with clients and 3 hours to complete the analysis and documentation.)

   - The resulting schedule is highly dynamic, based on your SMEs' availability and other priorities by the client. However, deadlines can be set.

Outcome: Project Discovery Schedule

These sessions serve as the backbone of requirements gathering and analysis, providing the groundwork for understanding, documenting, and prioritizing the business events identified.

Establishing a Structured Approach

Planning detailed discovery sessions requires a structured approach to ensure efficiency, effectiveness, and alignment with project objectives. This entails defining clear objectives, timelines, and resource allocations for each session. By establishing a structured framework, project teams can streamline the discovery process, maximize stakeholder engagement, and accelerate decision-making.

Creating the Schedule

Based on the Project Business Event List, a detailed schedule for the discovery sessions must be created. A schedule is set for each of the business events on the list.

This schedule includes the SMEs required for each business event session and the estimated time needed to complete the business requirements analysis. Key considerations include the availability of subject matter experts (SMEs), dependencies between business events, and project milestones.

Aligning with Project Objectives

Each discovery session should be aligned with the overarching objectives of the project, focusing on uncovering insights that contribute to value delivery and organizational goals. By clearly articulating the purpose and expected outcomes of each session – based on the context of the discovery session – project teams can ensure that stakeholders remain engaged and invested in the discovery process. This alignment helps to maintain momentum, eliminate scope creep, and drive consensus on project priorities.

Leveraging Standard Metrics

A standardized approach to resource allocation and session planning can enhance consistency and predictability across discovery sessions. Adopting a standard metric, such as allocating 4 hours per business event (1-hour session + 3 hours for the remaining detailed decomposition of the output from the one-hour session with SMEs), provides a baseline for estimating time and resource requirements. This metric helps project teams to manage expectations, optimize resource utilization, and maintain a steady pace of progress throughout the project lifecycle. This metric has been based on over 850 projects, large and small, by our consultants.

Managing Flexibility and Adaptability

While it's essential to establish a structured yet agile framework for planning discovery sessions, it's equally important to remain flexible and adaptable to changing circumstances. The project environment is dynamic, with unforeseen challenges and opportunities emerging as you progress. Project teams should be prepared to adjust the schedule, or reprioritize business events as needed to accommodate shifting priorities and stakeholder requirements.

Allocating Time and Resources

Using a standard metric of 4 hours per business event helps in planning the necessary resources. This includes an up-front 1-hour discovery session with SMEs and a subsequent 3 hours for decomposition and documentation of the details. This metric provides a clear and consistent approach to planning the discovery sessions, ensuring that sufficient time and resources are allocated to each business event. It also helps to manage expectations and ensure that the project stays on track. We have found that this 4-hour total meets pretty well all needs, whether the business event is large and complex or small and simple. Obviously, the smaller and more straightforward the business event being analyzed, the less time it takes, and the greater the accuracy. The front-end one-hour is always accurate, but the 3-hour detailed decomposition time can vary slightly, usually based on the complexity of the business event under analysis. But it always works out as an average 4-hours total, based on over 850 projects of data collection.

Engaging SMEs and Stakeholders

SMEs play a pivotal role in the success of detailed discovery sessions, providing valuable insights, domain expertise, and contextual understanding of business processes. Engaging SMEs early in the planning process ensures their commitment and availability throughout the sessions. Additionally, involving stakeholders in the planning phase helps to align expectations, clarify objectives, and secure buy-in for the discovery process.

Facilitating Collaboration and Communication

Effective collaboration and communication are essential for planning successful discovery sessions. Project teams must establish clear channels of communication, facilitate regular meetings and updates (much of which can be done virtually), and foster a collaborative culture that encourages sharing of ideas and feedback. By creating a supportive and inclusive environment, project teams can harness the collective intelligence of stakeholders and SMEs to drive meaningful insights and outcomes.

Outcome: Project Discovery Schedule

The Project Discovery Schedule provides a roadmap for conducting the detailed discovery sessions, ensuring that all business events are covered. The schedule must be regularly reviewed and updated to reflect any changes or issues that will arise during the project.

Dynamic and Iterative Planning

The Project Discovery Schedule serves as a roadmap for conducting detailed discovery sessions, guiding the sequence, timing, and focus of each session. By maintaining flexibility and adaptability, project teams can respond proactively to emerging opportunities, ensuring that the discovery process remains aligned with project objectives and stakeholder expectations.

Ensuring Comprehensive Coverage

The Project Discovery Schedule provides assurance that all business events are covered systematically and comprehensively. By mapping each session to specific business events identified in the Project Business Event List, project teams can track progress, identify gaps, and prioritize activities effectively. This comprehensive coverage minimizes the risk of overlooking critical requirements or dependencies, ensuring that the project delivers maximum value to the organization.

Facilitating Stakeholder Engagement

The Project Discovery Schedule also serves as a communication tool for stakeholders, providing visibility into the timing and scope of upcoming sessions. By sharing the schedule with stakeholders, project teams can solicit input, address concerns, and align expectations regarding the discovery process. This proactive engagement helps to build trust, foster collaboration, and enhance stakeholder satisfaction throughout the project lifecycle.

Planning detailed discovery sessions is a critical step in the project lifecycle, laying the foundation for effective requirements gathering, analysis, decomposition, and prioritization. By adopting a structured but agile approach, leveraging standard metrics, and engaging stakeholders and SMEs collaboratively, project teams can ensure that the discovery process is thorough, efficient, and aligned with project objectives. The Project Discovery Schedule serves as a dynamic roadmap for conducting sessions, determining participants, and tracking progress, ensuring comprehensive coverage of business events and maximizing value delivery to the organization. Through proactive communication, flexibility, and adaptability, project teams can navigate the complexities of the discovery process successfully, driving meaningful insights and outcomes that contribute to project success and stakeholder satisfaction.

---

4. **Conduct Detailed Discovery Sessions.**
   - Based on the *Project Discovery Schedule,* invite the identified subject-matter experts (SMEs) and conduct interactive one-hour discovery sessions for each *business event* to complete the business requirements for the project.

   - Complete the remaining documentation for each *business event.*

Outcome: Project Business Requirements

These detailed discovery sessions are where the bulk of the business requirements analysis takes place. This is where there's most interaction with subject-matter experts (SMEs), and where the vast majority of functional business requirements are discovered. This is where the most valuable contributions come from SMEs and stakeholders, and opportunities are uncovered. This is the centre of the universe of business system requirements analysis.

Inviting SMEs

Based on the Project Discovery Schedule, the SMEs identified as contributors to specific business events are invited to participate in one-hour interactive discovery sessions.

Conducting the Sessions

An experienced and proactive business analyst (the "pilot") leads the discovery session. The "co-pilot" (another analyst) captures all the resulting documentation for each business event – the process, objects, data, business rules, narratives, and notes. These discovery sessions are brief (one-hour) and highly focused on discovering the process and data needed to support specific business events (a situation, circumstance, or condition the business needs to respond to). Based on the knowledge of the SMEs, the applicable business rules are identified and allocated to the data that interacts in each business process.

Completing Documentation

Completing the documentation for each business process associated with one or more business events happens in two stages. The first stage is during the discovery session when interactions are happening. At this time, the co-pilot captures the process diagram, the supporting objects and data, the business rules associated with data and process interaction, and a descriptive narrative of the business process. This is all part of the one-hour discovery session with SMEs.

The second part of this is during the further decomposition of each business process, which is done offline from stakeholders (but they can be contacted for questions). On average, 3-hours is allocated to this analysis. It consists primarily of decomposition of the objects, data, business rules, and process narratives uncovered during the interactive session with SMEs. This usually expands the earlier work, but does not change it fundamentally. It sometimes leads to the discovery of new or previously undiscovered business events, which then have to be added to the schedule.

Outcome: Project Business Requirements

The Project Business Requirements document is a comprehensive compilation of all the business requirements gathered during the discovery sessions. It serves as a reference throughout the project, ensuring that all team members and stakeholders are aware of the business requirements, and that solutions – including technology solutions – will be designed and implemented for each of them as the project progresses. Stakeholders and SMEs have already been part of the individual discovery sessions, so the approval process (yes, there has to be one) would be quite straightforward.

Cultivating a Culture of Continuous Improvement

Detailed discovery sessions present an opportunity not only to capture immediate requirements but also to foster a culture of continuous improvement and learning. By soliciting interactive feedback, reflecting on process effectiveness, and identifying areas of opportunity and enhancement, project teams can iteratively refine their approach, driving greater efficiency, innovation, and stakeholder satisfaction.

---

5. Coordinate Business Analysis Completion.

- Depending on your mandate, you – as the business analyst and "Pilot" for the project – will coordinate completion of the business analysis part of the project. The project may be phased or staged, which usually means you will "Pilot" each stage of business analysis.

- It will almost certainly extend into the solution design or software acquisition stage. If this is the case, it would be most productive if you were part of the team guiding the technology team through the business requirements.

- Lessons learned from all the discovery sessions are also integrated and documented now.

Outcome: Business Analysis Project Review

This is the end-stage of the front-end project within a project – the business requirements analysis project.

Managing the Project Phases

As the project "pilot," the lead business analyst oversees the completion of each stage of front-end business requirements solicitation and documentation. Once this phase has concluded, it may involve coordinating with the technology team during the solution design or software acquisition stages. The business analyst should ensure that all aspects of the business analysis are completed on time and to the required standard. This includes managing any issues or risks that may arise and ensuring that all necessary documentation is completed and validated.

Coordinating with the Technology Team

If the project extends into the solution design or software acquisition stage, the business analyst should be part of the team guiding the technology team through the business requirements. This ensures that the technology solution aligns with the business requirements and that any issues or gaps are addressed. The business analyst should work closely with the technology team, providing support and guidance as needed.

Documenting Lessons Learned

Integrating and documenting lessons learned from the discovery sessions helps to improve future projects. This includes identifying what worked well and what could be improved, as well as any issues or challenges encountered. This documentation should be reviewed and shared with the project team and stakeholders to ensure that lessons learned are applied to future projects.

Outcome: Business Analysis Project Review

The Business Analysis Project Review summarizes the project's findings, successes, and areas for improvement, providing valuable insights for future projects. This review should be comprehensive and detailed, including all aspects of the project and the business analysis. It should be shared with the project team and stakeholders to ensure that all lessons learned are captured and applied to future projects.

Leveraging Agile Methodologies

Projects today must be able to respond quickly to change and even uncertainty. Agile methodologies enable this better than the methods of the past – as long as the target is completion of the work rather than reams of documentation. Documentation *is* important (it's the memory of the requirements), and it should form part of the process of requirements elicitation, not be something that's done after the fact. Nor should it slow down the elicitation process. It should be an embedded part of what's done, rapidly, and without undue bureaucracy.

By adopting an iterative, recursive, and incremental approach, a project team can respond swiftly to evolving requirements, mitigate risks, and accelerate value delivery. There is no doubt that agile methodologies promote collaboration, transparency, and stakeholder engagement, fostering a culture of continuous improvement and innovation.

Cultivating Cross-Functional Collaboration

Effective business requirements analysis requires seamless collaboration between cross-functional teams of stakeholders. By fostering a culture of collaboration and knowledge sharing – which can be supported by open and transparent discovery sessions with SMEs and stakeholders – project analysts can benefit from the collective expertise of SMEs with diverse perspectives, which drives innovation and resilience. Moreover, by leveraging an approach that is collaborative (evidenced by group discovery sessions), project analysts will streamline communication, facilitate decision-making, and enhance productivity.

Prioritizing Stakeholder Engagement

Stakeholder engagement is literally the most important aspect of the success of business requirements analysis. Stakeholder and SME engagement ensures continual alignment with organizational goals and objectives. By actively involving stakeholders throughout the project lifecycle, using highly interactive discovery sessions, project analysts will be able to get accurate and complete feedback, address issues and concerns, and foster buy-in. This drives stakeholder satisfaction and project success. Moreover, by leveraging insights from stakeholders and SMEs, project analysts can identify emerging opportunities, mitigate risks, and optimize outcomes.

Coordinating the completion of business requirements analysis for any project, large or small, is the culmination of meticulous planning, strategic execution, and collaborative effort. All of this. But without pain, unnecessary bureaucracy, reams of old-school documentation, or large teams taking the old Waterfall approach by default.

As the steward of project success, the lead business analyst (the "pilot") assumes a pivotal role in bringing together seamless integration across the project, effective collaboration, and highly focused documentation. By coordinating with cross-functional cohorts of stakeholder and SMEs, and documenting lessons learned, the "pilot" analyst lays the groundwork for informed decision-making and continuous improvement. Moreover, by leveraging agile methodologies, cultivating cross-functional collaboration, and prioritizing stakeholder and SME engagement, project teams can enhance the agility, resilience, and effectiveness of business analysis completion. In essence, by embracing a strategic approach and harnessing the collective intelligence and expertise of stakeholders, project teams can navigate the complexities of business analysis completion with confidence and achieve meaningful outcomes that propel the organization towards success.

The 5-Point Project Plan – Conclusion

The 5-Point Project Plan provides a structured and systematic approach to uncovering and specifying business system requirements – yet dynamic and agile.

By following this plan, businesses can ensure that their projects are well-defined, stakeholders are engaged, and objectives are met. The Plan's emphasis on detailed planning, stakeholder collaboration, and thorough – but brief – documentation ensures that business requirements are accurately captured and effectively communicated, leading to successful project outcomes. This approach helps to build a solid foundation for the project, ensuring that all necessary aspects are covered and that the project stays on track.

Review – The 5-Point Project Plan

> *"If you don't know where you're going, you'll end up someplace else."*
> – Yogi Berra –
> American baseball player, manager, and coach.

The 5-point project plan is designed to be specific to the front-end business requirements analysis of a project.

Any plan to uncover and specify business system requirements must be <u>specific</u> and <u>measurable</u>, not just another item on the list to be checked off. A plan must clearly identify what's to be done, by whom, and when. It must specify accurately the time and schedule involved. And it must be measurable – or it's just more of the Same Old Stuff made up of guesswork, magic numbers and unicorns.

1. **Initiate & Plan.** Working with your client …
   - Identify the "pilots" and "co-pilots" for the project. If you are the senior analyst on the project, then you're the "pilot".

   - Assignments include analyzing and documenting the project rationale, mandate, perceived scope, stakeholders, subject-matter experts, discovery session schedules, identified risks, expectations, and budget for the project.

- You'll also want to define the metrics required to measure project "success", and the acceptance approval process for the business requirements.

- Also, create a detailed list and definition of the deliverables and artifacts expected from the business requirements segment of the project.

Outcome: Business Analysis Plan

2. Conduct Project Scope Blitz.

- Even if your client believes they have the scope all figured out, you will still need to conduct a *Project Scope Blitz* for stakeholders and SMEs.

- This will require a ½-day or a full day. This highly interactive discovery session identifies the conditions and circumstances the business must deal with (for your project), at a workable *business event* level, as well as the business areas and departments involved at each stage of business analysis. It delivers a high-level, initial *Project Business Event List*. This enables you to schedule detailed discovery sessions. It also sets the tone for the project, right up front, and establishes your credibility as a business analyst.

Outcome: Project Business Event List

3. **Plan Detailed Discovery Sessions.**
   - Based on the *Project Business Event List*, create a schedule for each detailed discovery session and the subject-matter experts (SMEs) that are required to participate. Also, define the exact amount of time required to complete the project's business requirements analysis. (The metric we use in our organization is: 4 hours per *business event*, consisting of a 1-hour discovery session with clients and 3 hours to complete the analysis and documentation.)

   - The resulting schedule is highly dynamic, based on your SMEs' availability and other priorities by the client. However, deadlines can be set at this time.

   Outcome: Project Discovery Schedule

4. **Conduct Detailed Discovery Sessions.**
   - Based on the *Project Discovery Schedule*, invite the identified subject-matter experts (SMEs) and conduct interactive one-hour discovery sessions for each *business event* to complete the business requirements for the project.

   - Complete the remaining documentation for each *business event*.

   Outcome: Project Business Requirements

5. Coordinate Business Analysis Completion.

- Depending on your mandate, you – as the business analyst and "Pilot" for the project – will coordinate completion of the business analysis part of the project. The project may be phased or staged, which usually means you will "Pilot" each stage of business analysis.

- It will almost certainly extend into the solution design or software acquisition stage. If this is the case, it would be most productive if you were part of the team guiding the technology team through the business requirements.
- Lessons learned from all the discovery sessions are also integrated and documented now.

Outcome: <u>Business Analysis Project Review</u>

There is absolutely no need to make this more complicated than it is. The objective of front-end requirements analysis is to deliver value as quickly as possible to the client.

Book III

How to Run Awesome Business Discovery Sessions

How to Run Awesome

Business Discovery Sessions

Modern, Client-Interactive Requirements Analysis Sessions

What's this all about?

At the end of the day, the only way you can "do" Business System Analysis is to actually get together with clients, stakeholders, subject-matter experts (SMEs) ask them what it is they need for their system. Sounds straight-forward. But we all know it isn't. If it was, everyone would be doing it, without any big deal, and our business system requirements would be a breeze. But it just ain't so.

In our courses and seminars, we spend a lot of time addressing how to go about doing the business requirements analysis. We demonstrate. We do workshops. We deal with the theories and practices. We do more workshops.

But the reality is, a classroom or a seminar is not the real world. And we can never spend enough time on the foundations and principles ... the *"how do I do this?"* ... of sitting down with clients, stakeholders and subject-matter experts.

This section of this book ... is about the "how do I do this?" of sitting down with clients, stakeholders and SMEs, to figure out what they really want and need for their business system.

This section ... will put into context the nature of your questions, the environment you need, how long it takes, who should be involved, and the tools you need.

You'll also learn how to do it quickly, without missing a thing.

You'll really find out what "agile" means – with the results, the specifications, the documentation (sigh). But without the chaos.

So, let's get started.

What is a business discovery session?

A 'business requirements discovery session' is an interactive approach to conducting meetings with clients and subject-matter experts to probe and establish a project's business or organizational requirements.

These highly interactive sessions include clients, business partners, subject-matter experts, business analysts, executives and some system professionals. But not necessarily everyone at once.

These discovery sessions are based on the sound, old principles of analysis, but with greater flexibility and more suited to the 21st century. The Business Discovery Sessions we're going to explore are much more complete, and faster than conventional business system analysis.

What's a business discovery session good for?

Business requirements Discovery Sessions produce great savings by shortening the elapsed time required to gather business system requirements and by improving the completeness and quality of the requirements gathered.

This significantly reduces the number of costly downstream requirements changes.

Business requirements Discovery Sessions have been extremely successful with many organizations worldwide, private and government alike. Our consulting arm of our company has led thousands of interactive Business Discovery Sessions, and our consultants have led them on over 850 projects.

However, the success of a Business requirements Discovery Session is not just a function of the business analysis methodology you use, it requires a well-practiced professional to lead the sessions and the unreserved, enthusiastic participation of clients, business partners, subject-matter experts and executives.

In other words, there must be a real commitment by the organization's client base, not just fuzzy words of support.

"Real commitment" means putting in the time necessary to participate in Discovery Sessions.

To be clear, that "real commitment" is a lot less than the time required by conventional analysis methods.

There are two kinds of requirements discovery sessions: The **Project Scope Blitz** and the **Business Discovery Session**.

We will discuss both.

The risks and rewards of business discovery sessions

There are two major risks when planning requirements discovery sessions. Whether the discovery session is intended to be a front-end **Project Scope Blitz** or a series of regular **Business Discovery Sessions**, there are often unrealistic productivity expectations (a) before the discovery session, and (b) after discovery sessions.

When an organization embarks on a series of Business Discovery Sessions without being fully committed to the highly interactive nature of these sessions, it can fail or fall short of the mark.

But if an organization devotes the right amount of time and the right people, the results will be substantial.

The benefits of business discovery sessions

Some of the benefits of a Business Discovery Session include:

- It accelerates the business requirements learning process.
- It massively increases productivity by shortening the iteration cycle.
- It accelerates business revitalization and process re-engineering.
- It ensures the highest quality possible, because of direct participation by stakeholders and subject-matter experts.

- It ensures the most complete business requirements analysis in the shortest period of time.
- It helps to develop mutual respect between project business system analysts and clients.
- It provides a forum for exploring focused, in-context business revitalization ideas.
- It helps to deliver what the client needs and wants, quickly.
- It opens the door to success.

How the Business Discovery Session is conducted is what will set it apart from other approaches to gathering business requirements.

Critical ingredients for a successful Business Discovery Session include:
- leadership from a trained and experienced practitioner (a "pilot") <u>and</u> an expert scribe (a "co-pilot");
- participation by executive sponsors, key decision makers and *real* subject-matter experts;
- and the ability to work without the usual daily interruptions.

Business Discovery Sessions can last anywhere from an hour to several days, depending on the critical nature of the project. Discovery Sessions should be uninterrupted, as much as possible, since the absence of key people delays progress. Each individual Discovery Session is about an hour, but in some cases – for critical projects that need to get off the ground fast – several (or all)

Discovery Sessions for a project can be run contiguously – one after the other. This is both challenging and exhausting, but it enables the capture of all the project's business requirements faster than any other approach.

And what's a *real* subject-matter expert?

A *real* subject-matter expert (SME) has in-depth practical knowledge of the business areas affected by the project, and their work processes.

This person also understands why work processes are organized the way they are (at this time), and what these processes are intended to achieve.

This is not a surrogate "user"; nor is it a recent business school graduate who can fill the gap.

What is ... the project scope blitz?

Every project has to start with one of these. To make it work well, you have to gather all project stakeholders together for about a half-day. The objectives of a Project Scope Blitz are as follows:

- To quickly identify many of the *business events* that will be part of the target system. (I will define a *business event* soon.)
- To determine the business areas or departments that have responsibility for responding to and dealing with the identified *business events*.
- To accurately predict the amount of time required to complete the Business Discovery Sessions with clients

and subject-matter experts, and to prepare the Business Requirements Specification.

- To establish priorities – what *business events* will be done first, and which ones will be done later.
- To enable planning the schedule for Business Discovery Sessions with clients and subject-matter experts.
- To determine the effort and cost of the project's business system requirements analysis.

And ... what is a business discovery session?

For each *business event*, there will be a Business Discovery Session. The objectives of a detailed Business Discovery Session are as follows:

- To quickly get subject-matter experts on the same page, at the same time.
- To quickly uncover and discover the project's business requirements for one or more *business events* in a single session with one or more SMEs.
- To enable the business system analyst (the "pilot") to focus on a small component (a *business event*) and to quickly learn about the business requirements in support of that *business event*.
- To discover complete and accurate business requirements, focused and in context – not just "goodness and light".
- To get "buy-in" and ownership from stakeholders and SMEs.

- To develop and enhance mutual respect by all participants – subject-matter experts and business system analysts.

How long does a discovery session take?

Project Scope Blitz sessions usually take about a half-day, sometimes a little more. For an average project, if the client has a good handle on what they need, a half-day session is often enough.

It's important before planning a project's several Business Discovery Sessions to estimate how many *business events* there will be and how much time is needed for each one. How do you do that? Well, we'll discuss that a little later.

You also need to know who should participate – clients and subject-matter experts.

The project scope blitz

The **Project Scope Blitz** is very interactive with clients and subject-matter experts. It involves extracting from them the things they believe should be within the scope of the project.

Our experience is that the more senior the participants are, the better your results will be.

We'll look at what a *business event* is a little further on. For now, suffice it to say that a *business event* is a situation, condition, circumstance or external requirement. **It is not a process**. A process is what we do to support a *business event* – a specific situation or circumstance that your system has to deal with.

When you start up a **Project Scope Blitz**, you can start by asking the participants about some of the things they need to have in their new business system.

Their answers will not be in the form of *business events*. It's up to you, as the "pilot" analyst, to distill what they say and turn it into *business event* statements.

Each time you identify a *business event*, it must be listed and clearly displayed so the participants can see what you are doing, and they can read the *business event* statement as you have written it.

My preferred method is to write the *business event* statements with a dry-erasable marker on *Write On – Cling On* sheets which stick to the wall. You can Google this to find out more.

You can also use higher technology, involving a projector. As you capture the *business event* statements, you can project them onto a wall for everyone to see.

Either way, everyone gets to see what's being documented, which is really important.

They get to see what you hear.

One approach that I recommend when conducting a **Project Scope Blitz** is to create a short list of *business events* yourself, in advance, and then present these as "potential events" to your clients and subject-matter experts.

It's very important to suggest them strictly as "potential events" since participants are more likely to buy-in to their own knowledge and contributions than to yours. This approach is particularly useful if you don't have much information about the project, or when the project deals with something that's new or different.

The whole idea behind this use of "potential events" is to stimulate participation from your clients and subject-matter experts who are part of the Project Scope Blitz.

In the early part of any interactive session, people are often hesitant to say anything or to get the ball rolling.

If this is the case, then it's easy for you to toss out a "potential event" and to ask participants if that *business event* is something that could be part of the scope of the project. The answer could be a blunt *"no"*, in which case you strike it from your list.

If you would like to receive a set of about 4,000 business events from over 850 projects, organized by business type, just send me an email to trond.powerstartgroup@gmail.com.

After completing a Project Scope Blitz, you will have either a long or short list of *business events* for the project. There's no doubt you will <u>not</u> have discovered all of the required *business events*, but you will have enough to get you started.

Graphically, it would look like the picture below.

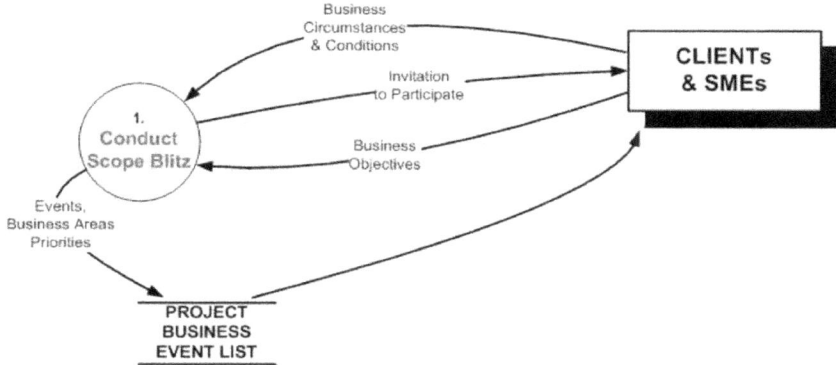

The process is as follows:

1. Determine the best time to conduct a **Project Scope Blitz**.

2. Issue a **Scope Blitz Discovery Invitation** to all clients and prospective subject-matter experts.

3. At the scheduled time, conduct the **Project Scope Blitz** with clients and subject-matter experts.

4. During the **Project Scope Blitz** with clients and subject-matter experts, determine the *business events* that are in-scope (as many as possible, but apply the 80/20 Rule, since other *business events* will be found during the detailed Discovery Sessions).

5. Record *business events* that are mentioned but are out-of-scope.

And, finally, issue the **Project Business Event List** to all participants as soon as practical after the **Project Scope Blitz**.

The Blitz itself should take half-day or a full day. It is very, very rare that it takes more time.

The business discovery session

Once the **Project Scope Blitz** has been done, you will need to plan and schedule the **Business Discovery Sessions**.

This can get very interesting since you'll have to deal with the random availability of people and coordinating the attendance of (usually) several people ... which means juggling vacations, conflicting meetings, time in the elevator, and more.

If you found, let's say, 30 business events in the **Project Scope Blitz**, you'll have to schedule 30 different **Business Discovery Sessions**.

To do this right away is not reasonable, so ... don't do it.

Based on the priorities established, I usually schedule no more than 3 or 4 at a time. This lets some of the dust settle as we discover details of the processes needed to support the different business events.

Graphically, it looks like the diagram on the next page.

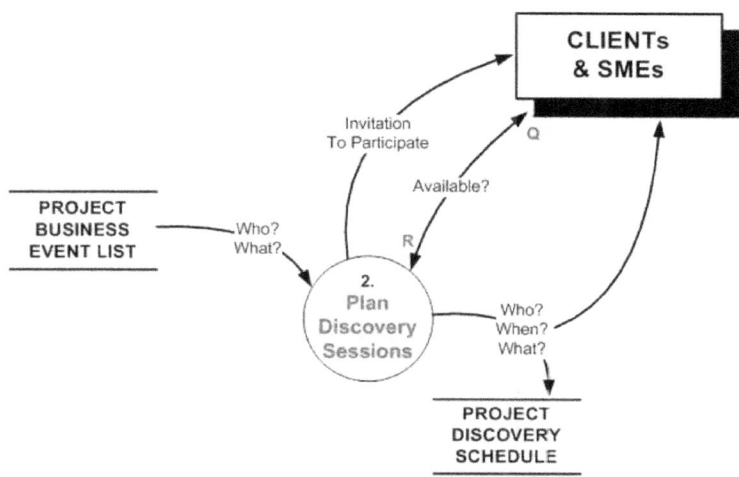

The planning process is as follows:

1. Based on the **Project Business Event List** you produced from the **Project Scope Blitz**, determine the availability of clients and subject-matter experts to participate in the detailed client-interactive Business Discovery Sessions for the project.

2. Create a **Project Discovery Schedule**, with participants and dates, for each *business event* on the **Project Business Event List**. Don't plan your entire list. That will only cause chaos, confusion and lots of rework later on. Just do 3 or 4 at a time.

3. When the schedule is complete (for 3 or 4 at a time), issue the Project Discovery Schedule and a formal "Invitation to Participate" in the Business Discovery Sessions to affected clients and subject-matter experts.

Follow-up with everyone by phone (not just email or text) or with a personal meeting. If some are participating by Zoom or some other form of video call, follow up with a personal phone call. It is very important that participants feel these Discovery Sessions are really important. Their success depends very much on their active and personal participation.

For each *business event* in the project, you will need to schedule a single **Business Discovery Session** for <u>one (1) hour</u> with stakeholders and subject-matter experts, regardless of the perceived complexity (or simplicity) of the process that supports the *business event*.

Your plan should provide for an **additional three (3) hours** per *business event* to complete the documentation. This is because there may be remaining work to be done outside the actual Discovery Session.

These metrics are based on over 850 projects our consultants have done, and the numbers are solid and predictable.

The one (1) hour interactive session with stakeholders and subject-matter experts tends to be quite precise, particularly when these sessions are led by a "pilot" analyst who has more experience conducting these sessions.

The three (3) additional hours per *business event* to flesh out and complete the remaining details is the average, but we have found it varies from 30 minutes to several hours more, depending on complexity and the type of project.

However, by planning for three (3) additional hours per *business event*, you'll be right on target at the end.

How much time is needed for a project's business requirements?

An "average" project, we have found, is between 25-75 *business events*.

A "small" project is less than 25 *business events*.

And a "large" one is over 75 *business events*.

Based on needing one hour of discovery time per *business events*, a "small" project will take up less than 25 hours of stakeholder and subject-matter experts. An "average" project needs between 25 and 75 hours with stakeholders and SMEs. And a "large" project needs over 75 hours of their time.

> **Note:** There can be more than one lead analyst ("pilot") on a project. When coordinated properly, this can reduce the calendar time for the project.

For mission critical projects, detailed Discovery Sessions for a project can also be scheduled as one hour per *business event* on consecutive days, with all parties involved. This "complete immersion" approach is very effective (arguably the most effective approach), but also very exhausting for SMEs and the business analysts.

We must also consider that stakeholders and SMEs have their own work to do, and dedicating several full days to Business Discovery Sessions is often difficult.

Regardless of the approach you take – and I do recommend the scheduling of one-hour sessions – each *business event* needs an average of three (3) additional hours by the analyst to dig up more details with SMEs, and to complete the business requirements specification for each *business event*.

The detailed Business Discovery Session is a team activity (you, as "pilot", and a "co-pilot" on one cohort; and stakeholders and SMEs as the other cohort on the team); therefore, typical teamwork guidelines apply.

It usually takes a project team a couple of days of these Business Discovery Sessions to jell and to ramp up on foundation information.

What kind of facility is required?

Any room with lots of uncluttered wall space will do. The wall space is important so you can put *Write On – Cling On* sheets on them to draw the diagrams you need, so everyone in the room can see what has been done.

While there is lots of technology that can project the diagrams onto a screen or a wall, including *Smart Boards*, we have found the dynamics and comfort level of participants when using *Write On – Cling On* sheets and whiteboards can't be duplicated.

Participants should be seated comfortably with desk or table space.

Who should participate?

A detailed Business Discovery Session should include a number of key people. Each Business Discovery Session should include **stakeholders** and **subject-matter experts** who are crucial to the success of the project, including **senior managers**, other **business partners** with a stake in the project, **project 'primes'** and anyone else who has a good understanding of the project's objectives, business rationale, and re-engineering vision.

A business and its systems can only be as good as the dedication and participation shown by its owners and stakeholders. All participants in a Business Discovery Session must bring an open mind.

These Business Discovery Sessions enable participants to "liberate the mind" and potentially discover business re-engineering opportunities, including immediate opportunities for improvement. (An *Immediate Opportunity for Improvement*, or 'IOI', is an opportunity discovered during requirements analysis that can be acted upon almost immediately and can lead to substantial business process improvement and added value to the business.) These IOI's, often found in detailed Business Discovery Sessions, can be invaluable to an agile organization.

Participants in Business Discovery Sessions should include the following:

Who should participate? – the Pilot

Business Discovery Session Leader – The Pilot. The "Pilot" is an experienced business system analyst who leads and facilitates Business Discovery Sessions. I like to use the term "Pilot" because they must lead the session, keep it on course, and take it to its desired destination without problems.

Without a doubt, the "Pilot" is most important to the success of the detailed Business Discovery Session. The successful "Pilot" has an exceptional combination of skills.

- The "Pilot" must have excellent communication and cooperation skills.

- The "Pilot" must be able to deal with political disputes, power struggles and personality clashes, although this doesn't happen very often.

- The "Pilot" needs to be completely impartial, with no political baggage, and be able to keep an open mind while managing conversations.

- The "Pilot" must be sensitive to hidden agendas and be able to redirect them constructively.

- The "Pilot" must be able to bridge communication gaps – technical, linguistic, and cultural.

- The "Pilot" must be comfortable speaking to and managing a group of people that often includes senior executives.

- The "Pilot" must encourage quiet group members to contribute their thoughts, and manage the strong personalities that sometimes dominate sessions.

Achieving all of this is not for the faint-of-heart. Therefore, the "Pilot" must have the respect of those who participate in Discovery Sessions.

That respect is earned through a series of successful detailed Business Discovery Sessions, but it also comes from general comportment, dress, civility, respect for participants, and being non-judgmental of contributions.

My experience is that when a Business Discovery Sessions fails, it is almost always because of the session leader or facilitator.

One of the reasons for session failure is when an organization wants to train a large number of people as "Pilots", but they lack sufficient recognition of the value of experience.

Some managers (thankfully, not too many) believe they can assign a new "Pilot" to a project immediately after a candidate has finished an analysis course of study.

Unfortunately, the result of trying to get everyone up to speed immediately, without the blessings and pain of experience, is that almost no one gets there.

This, in turn, can lead to unskilled "Pilots" and weak results. Weak results can lead to backsliding to the endless search for an analysis methodology "that works".

Of course, the methodology works just fine. Problems are usually the result of "Pilot" error.

It is my opinion that an organization that intends to use this approach to business system analysis should train, and support, a small core cohort of expert "Pilot" practitioners.

These "Pilots" should conduct as many Business Discovery Sessions throughout the year as possible. Our experience is that it takes about four projects for a new "Pilot" to become reasonably proficient. And they quickly get better after that.

Who should participate? – the Co-Pilot

Expert Scribe – The Co-Pilot. The "co-pilot" must truly be *expert*. The "co-pilot" can't just be the next available body. They must be fully trained in business requirements analysis and how a Business Discovery Sessions is run. They must know what they are hearing when they hear it – such as Objects, data attributes, and business rules. And they must have the knowledge and ability to back up the "Pilot", if required. We call this person a 'co-pilot' for just that reason.

The primary role of the "co-pilot" is to record what is said and done in the detailed Business Discovery Sessions. As such, this person will actively participate to make sure everything that's said and done is clear and concise.

Sometimes a "Pilot" is their own "co-pilot". Yes, really. This is the famous "team" of one person. It means the Pilot/Co-pilot, as the same person, wears a different hat at different times. However, if a "Pilot" is supported by a different person acting as "co-pilot", the time it takes to complete all the requirements documentation for the project is about half of what's needed if the "Pilot" works alone as both Pilot and Co-Pilot.

Who should participate? – the Coach

An Expert Coach. For the first four projects we recommend that an analyst be supported by an expert coach: Someone who is expert at running these Business Discovery Sessions and with business requirements analysis.

Having a coach who is experienced with these Business Discovery Sessions will lead to mastery of the methods and project success much faster, and with fewer challenges. This approach is a common practice in almost all professions and trades. It is time that we assured our own success by applying this best practice.

If having an Expert Coach onsite for the first few projects is not feasible, this kind of coaching can also be done remotely via Zoom or other video.

Who should participate? – Executive Sponsors and Project Primes

Executive Sponsors and Project Primes. If you want the project to succeed, make sure an executive sponsor or a fully empowered project prime participate in the **Project Scope Blitz**.

The <u>absence</u> of these people sends the message that the project isn't important enough for participation by other business partners, stakeholders, or subject-matter experts.

Executive sponsors and project primes are not necessarily the best people to participate in detailed Business Discovery Sessions, unless they are clear subject-matter experts.

Who should participate? – Subject-Matter Experts and other Business Partners

Subject-Matter Experts and other Business Partners. Get them involved as much as possible and as quickly as possible.

Involve stakeholders directly, especially the subject-matter experts (SMEs). Involve as many of the key people from the affected business areas and department as quickly as you can.

They should have a deep interest and enthusiasm for the success of the project. They should be the decision-makers, as well as the subject-matter experts (and these are sometimes the same people). Their knowledge of the business and their vision is instrumental to the success of the sessions.

Why do we need to do this?

Alright, why do we need to do this, when we could just conduct traditional interviews, or run good old fashioned JAD/RAD sessions?

First, interviews are impossible to make work effectively. We discussed this earlier. If you're not sure, go back and read it again. They take too long, sometimes are impossible to complete with all the SMEs on a project, and almost never enable cross-learning opportunities on new projects, thus enabling any kind of business process reengineering. Many of the subject-matter experts are in different office buildings and in different cities, which makes traditional interviewing on a project difficult and time-consuming – practically impossible, in my view.

Traditional interviews are dead in the water, in my opinion.

Second, good old-fashioned JAD/RAD sessions as simply that: Old-school, and much too rigid in approach. They are also much too focused on software design by committee, rather than trying to figure out what the actual business requirements are.

What do business discovery sessions accomplish?

Detailed Business Discovery Sessions accomplish any number of things, including the following:

(1) They enable better management of stakeholder expectations – because stakeholders are directly and actively involved in specifying the business requirements right up front. Since their involvement in producing the requirements is direct, and not just as "approvers" of the resulting document, they take ownership of the product based on the idea that most people don't disagree with themselves.

(2) They enable effective and efficient transfer of business knowledge from stakeholders and SMEs to the business analyst – again, because of their direct involvement.

(3) Business Discovery Sessions enable identification of important business *conditions*, *situations* or *circumstances* not previously mentioned or recognized by the client. These *business events* that were not previously recognized as within the scope of the project can include new opportunities for business revitalization not previously expected by the client.

(4) Business Discovery Sessions facilitate client 'buy-in' since they are directly involved in the discovery process of establishing the essential business processes, the data required to support those processes, and key business rules that govern the required behavior of the system.

(5) Client-interactive Business Discovery Sessions dramatically reduce the amount of time spent on identifying key business requirements.

(6) Client-interactive Business Discovery Sessions reduce software acquisition, development and implementation time considerably by removing ambiguity and ensuring fewer revisions (caused by omission) to the final requirements. In other words, it's faster by involving the stakeholders and subject-matter experts right up front and basing their involvement on individual *business events*.

(7) A client-interactive Business Discovery Session approach is essentially a **single-iteration approach**. What this means is that after one fast Business Discovery Session with subject-matter experts for each *business event* in the target system, the business requirements specification will be complete. No further revisiting, reiteration, rediscovery or redefinition of business requirements is necessary. A single-iteration (once through) approach to business system requirements means your analysis efforts are as fast as possible. This truly is the definition of "agile" within a no-risk paradigm.

So, what is a business event?

I've said a lot about *business events* in the context of Business Discovery Sessions. I can't just leave it there ... so, let's discuss what a *business event* really is.

A *business event* is an essential business condition, a state, circumstance, situation or requirement that exists – which the target system must respond to or deal with, in order to successfully support its key business objectives. A *business event* transcends time and technology. It does not reflect ***how*** something is done; it represents ***what*** must be done without regard to a particular technology.

To summarize, a *business event* is:
- a state, condition, circumstance, situation or requirement that exists;
- essential (critical) to the business; and

- based on time, a decision, situation or third-party need.

The four types of business events

Business events come in four flavors:

1) **Situation Business Event** – non-controlled
   "The Customer Buys a Product"
   "The Customer Has Exceeded Their Credit Limit"

2) **External Business Event** – based on third party need
   "The Customer Requests a Higher Credit Limit"

3) **Temporal Business Event** – based on time
   "The Customer's Credit Card Expires"
   "It is Time to Increase the Customer's Credit Limit"

4) **Internal Business Event** – based on a decision
   "The Company Decides to Cancel the Customer's Credit Card"

Note that a *business event* **never** starts with a verb. That's because a *business event* is not a process. A *business event* is a condition, state, situation or circumstance that must be supported by a process. A process ***does*** stuff. An event does not. It states the situation to be deal with.

For clarity – when a *business event* is identified we don't label it as one of the four kinds of *business events* listed above. We leave it unlabeled because, to a stakeholder or anyone else who is reading the documentation, a *business event* is simply a *business event*. It's a business circumstance. The four categories of *business events* exist to help the analyst to think about what kind of situation or circumstance they are really dealing with.

For example, what's the difference between **"The Company Decides to Pay a Supplier"** and **"It is Time to Pay a Supplier"**?

The first one – **The Company Decides to Pay a Supplier** – (an internal *business event* based on a decision) suggests that there is a decision point, and this decision must be reflected in the requirements specification.

The second one – **It is Time to Pay a Supplier** – (an internal *business event* based on time) suggests that there is no decision involved, it's just time to pay the supplier – perhaps the goods ordered have been received, or it's 30 days, and it is therefore time to pay the supplier.

By assessing the type of *business event*, the analyst is able to think through the ramifications on the business requirements.

The most common type of *business event* used by those who are new to this kind of analysis is the temporal *business event* that starts with **"It is Time to …"**. While this truly is a common type of *business event*, it is also the most common error, mostly because it is so easy to identify a *business event* as **"It is Time to … (something)"**.

For example, I have often seen *business events* such as **"It is Time to Receive a Product Shipment from a Supplier"** when it clearly should be **"Product Shipment Arrives from a Supplier"**. The arrival of the shipment from the supplier, while expected, isn't fully under our control, therefore it is an external *business event*. To state **"It is Time to Receive a Product Shipment from a Supplier"** seems a bit awkward and certainly doesn't have the same meaning as **"Product Shipment Arrives from a Supplier"**. On the other hand, a *business event* such as, **"It is Time for a Product Shipment from a Supplier to Arrive"** is something else again. This kind of *business event* is within our control, and we must have a planned response for it.

Thinking through the type of *business event* we're dealing with is therefore helpful in stating it well.

The symbiotic relationship between objects and processes.

Anyone who leads a detailed Business Discovery Session must not only uncover the project's *business events*, but must also be listening for the data required, so they can eventually develop the business process to support the *business event*.

Let's talk about that for a moment, since this all has to do with running strong and successful discovery sessions.

A business "process" is inseparable from "data" – they have a genuine symbiotic relationship. In other words, each *business event* (i.e., circumstance or condition) that needs to be supported by the target system (or business area) must be <u>dealt with by that target system in some manner</u> (i.e., a specific process). This always requires <u>the use of data</u> – either to retrieve some data or to record some data. It's impossible to have a process that doesn't involve retrieving, viewing or recording of data. It's equally redundant to have data that isn't ever involved in some kind of process – something has to happen to the data, otherwise why do we bother recording it?

So, for each business event, there must be a related business process. The business process must identify the data needed to support it.

For a full and complete discussion of a methodology to find and describe business processes and accompanying data, you can read my book *"**Rapid Agile Business System Analysis:** Fast, Agile, Measurable Results"*, which can be found on Amazon.

On the following pages are the steps any leader of a Business Discovery Session should go through:

Create a short list of potential *business events* for the project.

Identify as many as possible. Send me an email, and I'll send you a list of almost 4,000 business events from over 850 projects, organized by category.

After an initial list of potential *business events* has been created, pick one *business event* to start with and ask the subject-matter experts (the ones who have knowledge in the context of the chosen *business event*) the following question:

"What do we need to <u>know about</u> or <u>remember</u> in order to support this business condition or circumstance?"

The purpose of this question is to discover what data is needed to support the *business event*. To then find the data, we can do the following:

Look and listen for nouns.

The first place you can look is in the *business event* statement itself. It will consist of at least a verb and a noun or more. The <u>nouns</u> in the *business event* statement are usually data <u>Objects</u>.

Listen for nouns with "substance".

A data Object that supports a business process must have at least two data items. Less is just a data attribute. For example, would the noun "**CUSTOMER**" need several data items to describe it? Would we need to know the <u>*customer's name*</u>, <u>*address*</u>, <u>*phone number*</u>, and more? If so – and if there are at least two such attributes and characteristics – then we have a real data Object. If not, then we just have an attribute that belongs to some other data Object.

It follows that all nouns are not data Objects. Some are just data attributes that belong to and describe data Objects. Others are full data Objects. To know the difference, you must determine if the piece of data, the noun, can be further decomposed. If you can't further decompose it, it's a data attribute. If you can, it's a data Object. And data Objects are the "data" that's described in any business process.

Identify data attributes by listening for nouns that are not Objects.

Sometimes we just don't know where a data item belongs, simply because it's a stray with no identifiable home (another data Object). When a client mentions a series of nouns that are clearly data items but don't seem to belong to a data Object already defined, but are undoubtedly related – such as *customer name*, *address*, *phone number* – then we "roll up" a group of related data items to form a new data Object that hasn't yet been formed.

Ask the Inclusion Question (for Objects).

For every data Object that participates in a process that supports a *business event* ask the following question:

"If I know about {the OBJECT} what will it enable us to do that we could not do if we didn't know about it?"

Ask the Exclusion Question (for Objects).

For every data Object that participates in a process that supports a *business event* ask the following question:

"If we do not know about {the OBJECT} what will it prevent us from doing that we must be able to do?"

Each of these questions is asked in a client-interactive Business Discovery Session. These Business Discovery Sessions with subject-matter experts focus entirely on the business requirements and not on system solutions or design. In Business Discovery Sessions, answers to questions asked of SMEs by a "pilot" analyst are captured by the "co-pilot"analyst for each process that supports a *business event*.

Business Discovery Sessions with subject-matter experts are conducted on the basis of one or more specific *business events*.

For each *business event*, you will create some kind of business process diagram. It really doesn't matter what kind or style, as long as you're comfortable, and your stakeholder community is also comfortable with your diagrams.

You'll do the process diagram, identify supporting data Objects, populate the data Objects with data items, and determine business rules specific to the business process. All of this will be done with the direct interactive participation and contribution of your subject-matter experts.

And then we're done ...

As soon as possible after you've wrapped up a Business Discovery Session with subject-matter experts, and you have cleaned up the resulting specifications and documentation – issue the business requirements dealing with the *business event* to all the stakeholders and subject-matter experts who participated in your discovery session.

"As soon as possible" could be the same day, but it's certainly within a day or two. The sooner it's done, the more responsive you'll be seen to be, and the more enthusiastic the response from your subject-matter experts will be too.

Three things are important in this very agile and lean process.

Three important things: First ...

First – Your documentation for a single *business event* should be very small. Typically, you will want to be asking them to review just 3 or 4 pages. You'll lose them if you have much more than that.

It will consist of about two pages describing the process that supports the *business event*. Put the process diagram on one page (on the left) and the process narrative on the other page (on the right), if it doesn't fit under the diagram.

For each of the data Objects you identify in the process diagram, you need to have a definition, data attributes and whatever business rules apply. Since most process diagrams only have 3 or 4 Objects, usually not more than six, this makes the documentation pretty lean.

Once you've got this done for a process that supports a single, specific *business event*, send it to the subject-matter experts who participated in the Business Discovery Session. Ask them to read and review the document. Give them a deadline for feedback. Ask, clearly, if what you have sent them represents what you and they, your SMEs, discussed in the discovery session.

Three important things: Second ...

Second — What your SMEs receive should look exactly like the process diagrams you drew on the white-boards in the actual Business Discovery Session, just a little prettier ... so they will recognize what they are reviewing. Most of them will be very comfortable with this, since you have already spent some time on the business process and the business rules in the discovery session.

Also, all the information contained in the very slim document is <u>their knowledge</u>, not yours. They will recognize it as such.

Three important things: Third ...

Third — Your fast and timely distribution of the documentation means it's still fresh in their minds. As they read, they will recall what was discussed. This provides the continuity you need to get good feedback. It will also stimulate them to get the feedback back to you as quickly as possible.

I have found this to be an exceptionally fast, agile and lean way of getting good feedback quickly, and a good way of keeping SMEs involved past the actual interactive Business Discovery Sessions. It's a way of overcoming the "out of sight, out of mind" syndrome, which can have so much effect on project progress.

What tools can you use for documentation?

Let's get one issue out of the way. I am not a supporter of certain software (you know the kind) because every one of these applications is designed to help software engineers, not your business partners. What they see and what they get is totally alien to their own business world.

In terms of what works well, the most commonly used is still simple documents, emailed internally.

But, personally, I like Wikis.

I certainly recommend the use of an expert-moderated Wiki for any project.

Wikis are easy-to-use, collaborative and do not need to be serial.

Different people can work on different parts of the Wiki at different times. You can restrict access to any individual or groups you want. The most famous Wiki is of course Wikipedia, which really is a collaboration on thousands of projects.

A Business Area or Project Wiki is particularly good for teams that are dispersed across the country, around the world, or even in different offices across the city. Feedback can be almost instant, and knowledge can be contributed by the people who have the knowledge.

A Project Wiki has two lives.

- The first is when it is the knowledge repository consisting of the business requirements specification preceding software installation.
- The second is its life after the software is implemented.

The transition from a business requirement Wiki to a Project or a Business Area Wiki takes place when stakeholders and subject-matter experts start to maintain the knowledge contained in the business requirements as a <u>knowledge set</u> of the business areas. Since this includes all areas and interfaces, not just those features developed as software support, the Project Wiki becomes a teaching and learning tool for the affected business areas.

The intent of any Business Area or Project Wiki is to make changes easy to do, not difficult.

Traditional documentation is always difficult to maintain, and is never maintained very well, if at all. Traditional documentation, once it is completed, is often never looked at again. That's a terrible waste. And it's very costly to the project in the future.

When a Business Area or Project Wiki is developed this way, maintenance of the business documentation now becomes the responsibility of the client and the subject-matter experts in the different business areas. They are more likely to actually do this as the content of the Business Area Wiki is knowledge about their own

Business Area, and not software documentation as was the convention in the past.

Key success factors

So, let's talk about some of the things that will help you make a successful project.

There are many success factors that are unique to each particular Business Discovery Session. However, there are some generally accepted factors that apply to just about any kind of interactive session:

- Be sure that the project's executive sponsors and key stakeholders attend and actively participate in the initial *Project Scope Blitz*.

- Issue the Project Business Event List to everyone who participated in the *Project Scope Blitz* as soon as possible after the session is done. It should go out no later than a day after the discovery session.

- Set realistic expectations for the work to be done in the detailed Business Discovery Sessions, and a realistic schedule. In terms of the time required, plan on one (1) hour per *business event*, with clients and subject-matter experts (SMEs) participating, and an additional three (3) hours per *business events* to complete the detailed analysis and further decomposition. That will be fast, and realistic.

    As I mentioned earlier, you may not actually need the addition three hours for every single *business event*. For some, you'll be able to clean it up and get it ready for distribution in less than 30 minutes, but for others it could take 6 or even 12 hours, depending on what you discover in your post-discovery session assessment. The three hours is an average over all the *business events*. Therefore, if you have 30 *business events*, you'll need 30 one-hour Business Discovery Sessions with SMEs, and a total of 90 additional hours of finishing work. This metric, the result of tracking over 850 of our projects, enables you to make a reasonable prediction of time required immediately after finishing a Project Scope Blitz. That's a whole lot better than an out-and-out guess based on nothing better than thin air, and a song and a prayer.

- Be very visible by conducting Business Discovery Sessions with all the people required to be involved in a *business event*. Avoid one-person interviews. They are inefficient, take much too long, and hide your visibility. Visibility demonstrates that you are not only gathering the requirements, but you are *seen* to be gathering the requirements.

- If the project becomes a software acquisition or development project, make sure the software engineers (the programmers, database designers and system designers) know how to read the kind of business requirements you will produce (whether it is a document or a Wiki); and, if custom building the software, how to turn it into a solution design.

- Do a lot of Business Discovery Sessions, every chance you get; but perfect practice – with a coach and mentor for "Pilots" and "co-pilots" – works better than practice without guidance by an expert. Having a coach experienced in these kinds of Business

Discovery Sessions will lead to mastery of the methods much faster, and project success with fewer challenges.

Other general success factors include:

- Actively encourage everyone to participate. Instead of being just a facilitator, be a proactive "Pilot" and leader.

- Have well established and agreed upon objectives for each Business Discovery Session. Explain to participants how a discovery session will generally only deal with the specific *business event* scheduled and the business process, data Objects, and business rules needed to support it. Explain how you may find some new, previously undiscovered *business events*, but these will not be dealt with in their own discovery sessions. New *business events* discovered will be added to the Project Business Event (Parking Lot) and will be done at some later time in the schedule.

- Be unbiased and neutral about the business requirement. As a business system analyst, it is your responsibility to determine what the client needs to support the business. It is **not** the business analyst's job to assess the correctness or value of the client's requirements. (Some will disagree with me on this, but that's OK; they are allowed to be wrong.) While you may suggest a path for your subject-matter experts (by using questions rather than answers), it is the SME's responsibility to determine the business processes and data that add value to the business.

- "Keep it as simple as possible, but no simpler." (With thanks to Albert Einstein.)

- Keep focused on the objectives. Stay with the subject *business event*, and don't jump to other unplanned subjects. Use the <u>Project Business Event List (Parking Lot)</u> for new *business events* that come up in discussion.

- Lead the discovery process; and uncover the business requirements.

- Use your stakeholders' terminology. Avoid all forms of technobabble.

- Don't judge the SME's questions and answers. If you didn't understand what they said, or if it just sounded strange, ask them to help you understand their question or answer.

- Never fear that your questions will sound strange or uninformed. I've found that this is actually a good thing, even when I have to pretend to understand less than I actually do. People love to tell you about what they do and their responsibilities. They also love to tell you what they know. And that's what Business Discovery Sessions are all about: getting the expert knowledge from the subject-matter experts.

- Challenge the SME's thinking, but do not challenge the SME. Sounds good, but how do you do that? The first step is to never ask *"Why?"* when they give you an answer. "Why?" is not a good question to ask an adult. In effect, it asks them to justify or rationalize their answer, and they are not there to do that. If a senior manager says, *"We want a report on widgets sold in the northwest region,"* and you're not quite certain what this means, it's not a good idea to ask that manager *"Why?"* The answer you get is probably not what you're looking for. Instead, replace your desire to ask "Why?" with the following question: *"Jean, if we have the report on widget sales in the northwest region, what will that <u>enable</u> us to do that we have to be able to do?"* ... or, from another perspective, *"Jean, if we <u>don't</u> have the report on widget sales in the northwest region, what will that <u>prevent</u> us from doing that we must be able to do?"* You'll get a real answer with either of these questions (which are just two sides of the same coin). The answer you get will be the real *business event* that you're looking for.

- Be clear and understandable. Don't mumble. Use complete sentences consisting of both nouns and verbs, at least most of the time. Don't use technobabble or terms the subject-matter experts are not familiar with. Avoid using acronyms unless they are common to your industry (which means many others besides yourself must know the acronym).

- Make people feel good. The better they feel, the more readily they will participate in future Business Discovery Sessions. Be good finding.

- Smile. A lot. People respond a whole lot better to smiles, especially if the subject is serious and sometimes complicated.

- Have fun. Use your good sense of humor. If this is sometimes difficult for you, work on developing a sense of humor. It can be learned and become part of your personality.

- Listen... listen... and listen some more. What people say and what they mean are sometimes a little different. Keep really focused on what they mean. When you're not sure, ask them to *"help me understand that better"*.

- If you are asked a question, you must <u>always</u> respond to the participant's answer in some manner.

These are some of the key success factors. Undoubtedly, there are many others that apply equally well.

Business discovery session tips and techniques

These are some of the key success factors. Undoubtedly, there are many others that apply equally well.

On the Discovery Sessions

- When starting a Business Discovery Session, remember to ground the participants in the fact that you will be focusing on the **'WHAT'**, not the **'HOW'**. Keep reminding them of this if they drift into how things should be done (solution design) or other solution discussions.

- There's a basic principle I like to remind everyone of: "<u>Partition the effort to minimize complexity</u>." If the process underlying a *business event* is becoming too complex, and if your brain is about to explode, it's probably because the subject-matter experts are attempting to have a single process support several *business events*. While this is natural, try to keep it as simple as possible. Simple works. Don't try to make it more complex. Go with it until you know better. Don't speculate about what you don't know. Peggy Lee, a wonderful jazz singer from back in the day, once made the wonderful song "*Is That All There Is?*" very famous. Yes, often, that is all there is. Move on.

- Optics are important in Discovery Sessions. So, print legibly on the whiteboards or *Write On – Cling On* sheets, and use **red** and **blue** as alternating colors when drawing pictures during a Discovery Session. It helps with visual recognition of material for your subject-matter experts, the "co-pilot", and you, the "pilot". Stay away from the other colors, since most of them can't be seen very well from even a few feet away.

- After you've completed a Business Process Diagram with your subject-matter experts (it doesn't matter what shapes and diagrams you use), walk through (or talk through) the process as a wrap-up, so your SMEs can confirm its substance once again. It also enables your co-pilot to validate that everything has been recorded accurately.

- As the Pilot, periodically check to ensure that the co-pilot is keeping up with you. Before a Business Discovery Session, work out signals between the two of you so the co-pilot can indicate a need to catch up before moving forward.

- As the Pilot, listen for the co-pilot's fingers hitting the keyboard. If there is dead silence, take a break from the Discovery Session and speak with your co-pilot to determine if everything is OK – that the co-pilot is actually capturing the information as it arises during the Discovery Session. Also listen for the pace of keying; i.e., is the co-pilot still keying something while you are ready to move ahead to the next topic. Or, has keying stopped and it appears the co-pilot is also ready to move on. Team communication is as important between you and your co-pilot as it is between you and your SMEs. If you are your own co-pilot (sad sigh), only speak to yourself in your inside voice.

- Tracking requirements in a system can be done by identifying specific data items in data Objects that define a particular status (e.g., open, closed, approved, rejected, etc.). Attributing a *date/time* data item to each different status will provide a complete record of an instance of a data Object as it changes state in a system.

- Remember that an "inventory" is really a list of many instances of a particular data Object (like "**PRODUCT**"), each having its own unique identifier (also known as a "key"). If you are looking at inventory management *business events*, consider having a status data item in the data Object (e.g., *sold, available, returned*, etc.) with an associated *date/time*. This will easily provide the information needed to create reports, issue product reorders, etc.

- Avoid using soft words when discussing business processes in a Discovery Session. Soft words like "update," "modify," "process," and "handle" are words that are only meaningful (i.e., have a clear definition) to the speaker. Instead, use pointier words like "record" and "remember".

- Always remember to get your SMEs to provide a concise definition of a data Object. It ensures everyone has the same understanding of what the data Object represents. Interestingly, data Object definitions expand considerably during most Business Discovery Sessions, so don't be happy with the first definition you encounter. It will probably change as you progress with the Discovery Sessions.

- Always think of a data Object in the singular. It helps ground people in understanding the purpose of the business process without getting distracted by number of instances, time, etc. Also, we (people) are not very good at thinking through multiplicity. Stick to the singular.

- Always name a data Object in the singular, even though it represents all possible occurrences of the data Object, including its history. Your diagrams represent the business view of the information, not a database design view.

On the Co-Pilot

The co-pilot is as important to the success of a Discovery Session as the Pilot. They have different but equally important roles. The following notes are for co-pilots who work with Pilots by documenting everything as it happens during a detailed discovery session.

So, if you're a project co-pilot, here's some advice based on hundreds of projects' experience.

- **Ask the Pilot to explain your role.**

    Initially, as a co-pilot, people will wonder why you are there and what you are recording. Will their words be held against them? Are you a spy? Clarify that you are there to ensure that the information discovered during this session is appropriately documented. Let participants know that the Business Requirements will be produced as soon as possible after all the Discovery Sessions are done. If the Business Requirements, or some part of it will be distributed, let them know that too.

- **Listen, listen, and listen some more.**

    Often, there will be more than one conversation taking place. The challenge is to figure out which is the key one. Try to stay focused on the same dialogue as the Pilot is engaged in. Because the Pilot will likely be actively listening to a specific discussion, encourage others to speak up (at the right time) if you are aware of other side discussions taking place.

- **Seek clarification.**

    If there is something you don't understand, ask for clarification. Most people in the room don't expect you to be an expert in the business at hand. That's their job. Your role is to ensure that the facts, as well as the thoughts and concerns of the SMEs get appropriately documented. Consequently, if you do not understand, or if the discussion has gone off in several directions, it is absolutely appropriate to ask participants to repeat their words to ensure that the discussion is accurately documented.

However, as the expert co-pilot, there is an expectation that you will have some innate ability to hear all, understand all, and document all. Sometimes you may find that it is more appropriate to follow up with specific individuals off-line. Your good judgment is necessary.

- **Read back complex narratives or business rules for confirmation.**

    If a particularly complex business process has been under discussion for some time, it may be appropriate to request a break so that you can consolidate your notes. If you do, after the break read back the updated version of the narrative or the business rules to get everyone back onto the same page.

- **Define all acronyms.**

    If acronyms are used in the discovery session (and they almost always are), make a note of them and follow up with individuals off-line to ensure complete understanding. Ensure that full definitions of these terms are included at least once in the document. If appropriate, consider adding a glossary of acronyms as an appendix.

- **If participants wish to see what you're doing, share it with them on breaks.**

    Remember, the document you are preparing belongs to everyone in the room. It is the consolidation of all their thoughts, ideas and experience. If they want to grab a glimpse on a break, no problem; share it with them. This is an excellent opportunity to check with individuals one-on-one to validate specific comments in the document. This will also enhance their confidence that their words are being recorded appropriately and that a great deal of work is being done by you, the scribing co-pilot, as well as by the people in the room. Visibility comes in many ways.

- **Leave the diagrams for later.**

    A Business Process Diagram will likely change as you progress through the Discovery Session. Diagrams are often on whiteboards or on *Write On – Cling On* sheets on the wall. Once again, visibility of the work you do is very important. Use the diagrams to get the process narratives correct during the session. Once the process definition and diagram are stable, add the diagram to your documentation.

After the Discovery Sessions

- **Add the diagrams to your documentation.**

    Copy the diagrams from the whiteboards or *Write on – Cling On* sheets on the walls to your documentation during the consolidation period at the end of the day, when there are no subject-matter experts around. Since diagrams can change during a discovery session as you get more information, there will be no time for you to capture the diagrams (perhaps more than once) during the session. The fastest and easiest way to capture the diagrams is with your phone's camera.

- **Create a backup of the diagrams.**

    Before you move any of the diagrams on *Write On – Cling On* sheets, create backup copies by using your trusty digital camera or phone. Take photos of all the diagrams.

Other thoughts on business discovery sessions ...

Where appropriate, give key subject-matter experts an opportunity to "see" an early version of the documentation for a specific Business Process Diagram (which may support one or more *business events*). This gives them a sense of how much work is actually getting done. Visibility is one of the keys to success.

When reviewing specific documentation with a subject-matter expert, be prepared for some "wordsmithing". This is why you are reviewing it – to ensure that the way the information is documented is how they want it. "Wordsmithing" is a step in the ownership process.

As discussed earlier, consider posting individual processes and their supporting information as part of an internal Business Area or Project Wiki. The business processes should represent what the organization wants, without detailing how it will be delivered, and it should be a living document. As a Business Area or Project Wiki, it can be used by the client community as a teaching or training tool, and it can easily be maintained by the client community that owns the business processes.

More Tips and Techniques ...

Listening

During the detailed Business Discovery Session, concentrate on listening to what is being said. Business Process Diagrams and Object data attributes can be captured at the end of the day – they'll still be on the *Write On – Cling On* sheets when all the subject-matter experts have left. Also, most narratives can be constructed from a good diagram quite easily. Look to the data flows to find the tasks.

There is a lot said during the Discovery Session by the Pilot and by the SMEs themselves that will not appear on any diagram you create, but needs to be captured in your narratives. Concentrate on combining what you see on your diagrams with what you've heard, and you should be able to build a process narrative that accurately describes the process taking place.

Judgment

A large part of being an expert Pilot or co-pilot is being able to determine what needs to be captured, and to distinguish the needed data from other information that arises during the discussion. Often in a detailed Business Discovery Session, a SME will get caught up in an explanation that contains a lot of information which is not really applicable to the immediate work you are doing.

You are not there to capture full descriptions of the job functions of everybody in the room.

You only want to capture information that belongs to the project's business requirements. Any extraneous information captured means there is that much more for the readers of the document to wade through to get to the real requirements. And that's not a good thing.

However, you simply can't cut somebody off and tell them that the information they are providing, while it might be important, is not useful in the document. Use common sense – and be flexible. Sometimes, letting someone get off-track in an area they believe to be important, can actually be very productive. Listening is a proactive skill that also requires the good judgment to let someone be heard, even when there's not much direct value added.

Verification

As co-pilot, don't be afraid to interrupt, stop the discussion, and make sure that what you've captured is what has been said. The information that you are capturing must represent what was said – you are building the definitive record of the business requirements. If you're not sure, double-check with the people that know best – the subject-matter experts.

As the co-pilot be sure to discuss your 'interruption option' with the Pilot before the Business Discovery Session starts. Agree on the best way to verify your information where required, and try to stick to that method. Don't step on any toes.

However, do not interrupt the discussion to add your own two cents worth regarding the business process. As the co-pilot you are not one of the subject-matter experts – that's why they are in the room.

If you have a vested interest in the outcome of the session, do not agree to be the co-pilot. If you're talking, you can't be listening or recording, and you'll very quickly find that you're falling behind in the capture of information. Your writing will also be biased, even if it is unintentional.

Teamwork

As the co-pilot, you and the Pilot are a team. Do your best to use your knowledge of business system analysis to know the direction in which the discussion could be heading, so you're not caught by surprise. Be ready to read back anything you've captured, at any time.

As co-pilot, if you have any questions about what is drawn or annotated on a *Write On – Cling On* sheet, ask the Pilot right away.

Technical Details

The business requirements concern the "what" and not the "how". It is not a technical specification. It is a business specification. That being said, there are times during a Business Discovery Session when there are things mentioned that might not be considered to be business requirements, but might be information that's needed to populate the database once it is complete.

For example, let's say you're discussing gas tanks. A data Object called **GAS TANK** would have attributes such as *height, width, depth, location, weight, date entered into inventory,* and *capacity*.

One of the SMEs might say, *"Well, none of our tanks can hold more than 100 gallons. Ever."*

Although this is a piece of technical data (which is certainly implementation dependent, since it could change in the future), it could save some time at a later point in the project if this fact is noted now, and it won't take long to record it as part of the business requirements.

The way to get around the "physical" nature of this data is to just enter it as a note in the description of the data attribute (*capacity*, in this example), or add the comment "technical note".

Five Phrases

For the purpose of writing narratives for business processes, here are five phrases I have found invaluable to kick-start the building of a process narrative.

1. "For each …"
2. "Periodically …"
3. "Determine …"
4. "Remember (or record) …"
5. "Find (or identify) …"

Don't limit yourself to these particular phrases when building your narratives, but they may come in handy if you find you can't think of how to word what you've just heard.

In addition to the word "Find" another word that might be helpful is "Identify". For example, when making a sale you want to remember who made the sale, but you don't need any salesperson information and you don't need to record anything about the salesperson. In this case, you might simply write, "Identify the SALESPERSON who made the sale."

The Agile environment
'Agile' is a frame of mind, not a methodology

The real key to being a successful expert co-pilot is to practice what you've learned. You'll find that the more you scribe, the better you'll be, and the easier it is to hear everything that's being said.

You might even find, with lots of practice, that you can listen to two (or even three) conversations at the same time and pick out what's important in each of them. (Ideally, there should only ever be one conversation taking place in the room at the same time, but we all know that this isn't reality.)

Lastly, know the analysis methodology you're using. Internalize it. Because if you know how all of the information that you're hearing in a discovery session fits together, you'll spend much less time thinking about where to put what you've heard – and you'll miss less. Discovery Session participants will be absolutely amazed by how you can capture so much information, and that you can so accurately describe their business processes.

Above all, if you want to foster an agile environment, involve stakeholders and subject-matter experts in requirements discovery, and involve them a lot.

The resulting business requirements documentation should be in business language, and as brief as possible. And a stakeholder should not be expected to learn the technology you're using.

Recognize that you serve your client – whether that client is part of an internal group or a customer outside your organization – and you need their help and active participation to understand their business requirements.

Recognize that requirements will change as your stakeholders understands better the information they want and can have. It's not a bad thing to "change your mind" when you have more information. As the famous British economist John Maynard Keynes once said, *"When the facts change, I change my opinion. What do you do?"*

The issue is how to deal with those changes, since history tells us that change is good. This is what learning is all about, so when a stakeholder or subject-matter expert changes their mind, don't think *"not on my project."* This is actually a move in the right direction.

I believe very strongly that business requirements analysis should be focused on individual *business events*, and their supporting processes, rather than trying to write a novel about how a system should work.

By focusing on the individual *business event* and its supporting processes and data, you can respond very quickly to any change that is needed.

It minimizes the complexity of changing page after page in a serial novel. In event-based analysis, as I've briefly described it, there is no redundancy; therefore, there is no domino effect in the documentation. It allows the business analyst to respond rapidly, while it gives the client or subject-matter expert the confidence to contribute without fear of criticism of "constantly changing their mind".

In my opinion, "agile" means being fast and responsive, but without chaos and risk. An event-based approach to business requirements analysis is extremely fast, and without risk.

The alternative – conventional system analysis that usually takes a long time – often leads to abbreviated requirements analysis (*"we finished when we ran out of time"*), which in turn leads to incomplete work down the line, and perhaps costly rework later on.

The Professional's Success Code (Revisited)

Finally, let's talk about the professional's success code – the one that was outlined earlier in this book.

Bringing business professionals together with analysts in a modern and agile Business Discovery Session is the cornerstone of the environment you will create when doing business requirements analysis. This environment creates a dynamic and a "user buy-in" rarely seen before.

If you use highly client-interactive discovery sessions to help determine business requirements, my experience indicates that you will have great success uncovering business requirements quickly, accurately and completely.

The size of your organization doesn't matter. It will work very well in virtually any size of organization, government or non-government, given motivated individuals.

To be successful on the projects we take on we must not only have a good requirements acquisition methodology – one that supports agility and responsiveness without chaos and risk – we must have an agile approach to business requirements analysis that is predictable and repeatable as well.

What I mean by this is that every analyst who conducts Business Discovery Sessions should run them more or less the same way. So, cross-learning and internal mentorship is really important. This means that if different analysts conduct different discovery sessions on the same project, the results should have the same outputs and quality as if only one analyst was doing the work on a project.

Every professional must have a foundation that guides all system acquisition or development work.

Conclusion

A lot has been written – in many books, articles, and blogs – about what an 'agile' project is and what it isn't. It seems like you can put five people in a room and you'll get eight opinions.

One thing I'm sure of is that an 'agile' project or 'agile' environment is really a frame of mind, rather than a process. It's a paradigm or mental model of how we can approach our work. It's certainly not a methodology.

You'll get good at this. Practice. Just do it. Make mistakes. It's the only way we know of to become expert at anything.

If you have any questions …

Send me an email any time. I promise to get back to you as quickly as possible, time-zones notwithstanding.

I can't do your project work, nor will I comment on your specific project (except for a fee); but I can certainly answer some questions and provide guidance.

Please let me know your thoughts on this book and its subject-matter. And, of course, recommend it to others.

Come by and say hello.

Trond Frantzen
trond.powerstartgroup@gmail.com
powerstartgroup.com

Books by Trond Frantzen

Business System Analysis

- Managing Successful Requirements Projects: The Analyst's Playbook
- Agile Business Requirements Analysis
- How to Run Awesome Business Discovery Sessions
- Business Requirements Analysis Made Easy
- Mastering Business Requirements Analysis
- Process Modeling for Business Analysts Made Easy
- Requirements Analysis for Non-Technical Business Analysts
- Business System Analysis for IT Consultants
- Rapid Business System Analysis: The Course
- Rapid, Agile Business System Analysis
- How to Run Awesome Discovery Sessions
- A Game Plan for System Development (with Ken McEvoy)

Environment, Social, and Governance

- Your Politician & The Environment: How to Build a Sustainable Future (The Fight for Our Lives #3)
- Politics vs. Planet: The Battle for a Sustainable Future (The Fight for Our Lives #2)
- Clean Energy & Technology Innovation – and the Environment: Are They Sustainable? (The Fight for Our Lives #1)
- ESG: From Acronym to Action (with Chris D. Tesarski)

www.ingramcontent.com/pod-product-compliance
Lightning Source LLC
Chambersburg PA
CBHW071924210526
45479CB00002B/551